A Woman's Way

A Woman's Way
A Freedom Ride For Navigating Life's Highway

CLARE-ANN TAYLOR

A Woman's Way: A Freedom Ride For Navigating Life's Highway

Copyright © Clare-Ann Taylor, First published 2022

Clare-Ann Taylor asserts the moral right to be identified as the author of
A Woman's Way: A Freedom Ride For Navigating Life's Highway

Copyright © Clare-Ann Taylor Publishing

All rights reserved. No part of this publication may be reproduced, stored in a retrieval system or transmitted in any form or by any means, mechanical, electronic, photocopying, recording or otherwise, without the prior written permission of the author.

This book and any associated materials, suggestions and advice are intended to give general information only. The author expressly disclaims all liability to any person arising directly or indirectly from the use of, or for any errors or omissions in this book. The adoption and application of the information in this book is at the readers' discretion and is his or her sole responsibility.

National Library of Australia Cataloguing-in-Publication entry:
Taylor, Clare-Ann 2022 - A Woman's Way: A Freedom Ride For Navigating Life's Highway

ISBN: 978-0-646-86787-8

Editor: Lyndal Edwards
Photography: Jeff Darmanin
Artwork: Jorja Cummings

Dedication

Behold the mirror to your soul.
May it magnify your pure essence and
guide you towards your true magnificence.

To the sisterhood of women ...
may you be and feel seen!

INTRODUCTION   1

CHAPTER 1: THE DRIVER
Introduction   8
The Labels We Are Given   10
The Unwanted Label of Perfectionist   11
GPS: You Control Your Direction   13
The Fork In The Road   14
My Big Fat Fork In The Road   16
Your Fork In The Road   19

CHAPTER 2: THE DRIVER'S SEAT
Introduction   26
What Is The Value Of Values?   27
Living By Your Values   32
Choose Your Seat, Choose Your Values   33
Customise Your Seat, Customise Your Values   36
Your Number Plate   37

CHAPTER 3: THE WINDSCREEN
Introduction   42
Preparing The Windscreen   43
Goals & Systems   43
What Is A System?   44
Actions Speak Louder Than Words   52
Blurred Vision   54
Heart - Head - Hands Approach   55

CHAPTER 4: THE BAGGAGE
Introduction   62
What Is Excess Baggage?   63
The True Cost Of Our Excess Baggage   64
How Does Baggage Show Up In Life?   66
Internal Dialogue – Heart vs Ego   68
Key Reasons We Hold On To Excess Baggage   70
Preparing To Let Go   72
Getting Out Of Your Own Way   74
Minimise Baggage, Maximise Adventure   75

CHAPTER 5: THE BRAKES

Introduction	80
What Is Fear?	83
Fear vs Phobias	84
What Do We Fear?	85
Types Of Fears	86
Fear vs Worry	87
Facing Fear	89
Using Fear As An Engine	90
Facing Fear Head On	91

CHAPTER 6: SPARK PLUGS

Introduction	98
What Is A Spark Plug?	101
Finding Your Spark	102
What Does Your Spark Look Like?	104
Finding Sparks Of Joy	106
Joy vs Happiness	107
Tickles Of Joy	108
Jump Start Joy	109

CHAPTER 7: THE STEERING WHEEL

Introduction	114
What Does Purpose Mean?	117
How Do I Find My Purpose?	120
The Passion-to-Purpose System	121
What Is My Passion Or What Sparks My Curiosity?	121
What Is My Gift?	122
What Are My Skills?	123
Hang Out With People Who Are Following Their Purpose	124
Say Yes	125
How Do I Live My Purpose?	126
Realising and Embracing Your Road Map	128

CHAPTER 8: THE PASSENGERS
Introduction	136
What Are Passengers?	138
Long-term Friendships	139
The Magic Of Connection	140
What Is A Tribe?	141
Your Vibe Attracts Your Tribe	141
Tribal Member Qualities	142
Responsibilities As The Driver Of My Passengers	144
How Do I Find My Tribe?	145
Average Of The Five People	146
Hitchhikers	147
What Do I Do With My Tribe?	150

CHAPTER 9: THE FUEL
Introduction	154
Choosing Our Fuel	157
Maintenance Of Your Body, Mind & Spirit	159
Fuel Light	160
Maintaining Our Bodies	161
Listening To Our Bodies	162
Maintenance Specialists	164
Gratitude and Giving Thanks	164
Mind Matters	165
A Mind Under Pressure	166
Lift Your Spirit	168
The Gift of Giving Without Expectations	169

CHAPTER 10: PERMISSION GRANTED
Introduction — 176
Personal Definition Of Permission — 179
Where Independence Shows, Permission Grows — 181
What Are We Waiting For? — 182
Fear of Failure — 184
What Ifs — 185
Permission To Say No — 186
Permission To Invest In You — 186
Permission To Be Imperfect — 186
Women Leading By Example — 187
Permission To Let Go! — 189
Letter To Self — 192

FINAL THOUGHTS — 199
AUTHOR Q & A — 202
ACKNOWLEDGEMENTS — 204
REFERENCES — 206
ABOUT THE AUTHOR — 211

Introduction

Welcome to the sisterhood of intrepid adventurers!

I am your co-driver and motivational navigator. I am here to mentor you along the exciting journey which awaits you in *A Woman's Way*. Years of experience and gathered wisdom, both personally and professionally, have brought me to this role. I now feel ready and honoured to act as your guide. I'm here to help steer you on a journey of self-discovery, personal growth and freedom.

My desire to write *A Woman's Way* came about when I found myself stuck at a crossroad. I was on the cusp of turning 40, living an overly structured life and craving a more relaxed, bohemian lifestyle. From the outside I appeared a quietly confident, creative being who was kicking goals and living her 'best life'; but within, I was slowly suffocating beneath the ill-fitting mask of inauthenticity I awkwardly donned each day. All I craved was the permission to rip it off so that I could breathe deeply and freely.

I searched desperately for answers, but as my library of self-help books grew, so too did my discomfort in my world. Nothing seemed to shake my unease or lift my spirits.

My saving grace was a journal I kept which I aptly named Grace. The contents of Grace, and the practical exercises I share within *A Woman's Way*, became my faithful GPS to navigate through my chaotic gridlock of confusion.

The Kombi became the metaphor which drove my hopes and dreams.
It represented untold freedom, unleashed fun and unkept hair, so much so that it became the driving engine of this book.

Whilst I don't expect you to own a Kombi, nor am I insisting you purchase one (although that would be pretty cool!), I refer to you as the Kombi driver throughout these pages, to illustrate my message and immerse you in the whole road trip experience.

The German designed Kombi - official name Kombinationskraftwagen - translates as 'combination motor vehicle.' It's an iconic people mover and adventure mobile. What better choice of vehicle to move myself and my tribe through this journey I call life? Often likened to a 'loaf of bread on wheels', (as the Portuguese affectionately refer to it), the Kombi has long been associated with the flower power generation.

My personal connection to Kombis is simple - they make me smile. What they lack in power they ooze in charm, and as I'm in no particular rush to reach my destination, the Kombi and I are meant for each other.

As I write this book, I'm in search of an ever elusive automatic, dual coloured, 'splitte' (split windscreen), 1960's vintage Kombi. I have put my faith in the universe that she will steer me towards my dream car. While I wait, I'll keep busy making plans for my first real adventure!

A Woman's Way fulfils a ten year vision of mine, to create an inspiring journey for women of all ages - at any stage of life - to dive in deeply, stir things up, and create the most incredible roadtrip of change in their lives.

My personal journey has been filled with flaws and imperfections along the way. I now see that those imperfections have brought me to a place of inner peace and self-love; a place where I am in control of the choices I make, in response to the events and emotions I experience. Although my monkey mind still chatters, I welcome its noise as a reminder of the strength that I've gained and the growth I have experienced and created.

Over the years I've learnt that, like most women, I need to feel appreciated; both seen as well as heard. As an introvert, I spent those same years wondering how I could achieve this with the gentleness of a lamb and the voice of a mouse.
It wasn't until I fell upon the realisation that the women who inspired me most were the ones whose sheer aura captivated me and whose kindness embraced me.

The blessing of femininity conjures many emotions for me, as I know it will for you. For me, the pure essence of feminine energy exudes an eloquent strength of character with honest vulnerability.

There is true beauty in a woman's compassion, yet fierceness in her protective nature. Words need not only be spoken nor projected through loud hailers, for she is also seen and heard through her convictions and the warmth of her smile.

A *Woman's Way* is written for the sisterhood I have come to know and honour and the individual and powerful personalities that stand within that circle.
For all the women who journey into this book and are empowered by its teachings I applaud you for jumping into the driver's seat and investing in you. May the trail you blaze cast a glow so bright that your spark is seen, and your vibe felt by more people than you ever thought possible.

In structuring *A Woman's Way*, I wanted it to be read as a self guided manual - similar to that of a vehicle's operational manual - with a journaling component to maximise and deepen the experience of the content.

The Kombi forms the pivotal metaphor from which the chapters are driven.
Each chapter represents a specific part of the Kombi, with similarities drawn and connections made with particular aspects of our lives.

Whilst the chapters of *A Woman's Way* follow a natural flow, it doesn't necessarily need to be read in sequential order. There are no rules here!
After all, you are the driver, you can steer your journey in any direction you choose.

Peppered throughout each chapter are Ignition Exercises, designed to ignite and spark your thoughts and encourage your written reflections. I have hand selected exercises that I trust will tease your curiosity, deepen your thinking and empower your journey.

A Woman's Way is meant to be a light hearted approach to regaining control of your life, then finding your road to freedom, behind the wheel of your Kombi.

As your co-driver, I beg you to take yourself less seriously and live a little more adventurously. I have chosen to share many personal stories that pull back the Kombi curtain on my past, shed light on my present, and fuel up for an interesting future. I hope that you will do the same.

My wish for you is simple. I want A Woman's Way to be your personal guide, steering you towards a place where your true self thrives and your spirit soars; a place where you experience joy, realise your purpose, and create the most exquisite ride to empower yourself and impact those who matter most to you.

This is your journey, your time to step out of your familiar vehicle of life. It's your time to embrace the unknown of a new road ahead and reset your true GPS.

It's time to discover exactly who you are when you're in the driver's seat of your life with the wind in your hair!

Will it hurt? Not much. Will it be scary? Maybe a little.

I encourage you to allow yourself to be vulnerable, curious and most importantly authentic. Clear your windscreen, adjust your mirrors and buckle up for the ride of your life!

This is your journey, driven your way … A Woman's Way!

Sending you love and light!

Clare-Ann Taylor
xxx

November 2022, Australia

This is your journey, driven your way ...

A Woman's Way
xxx

*The search for a personal identity
is the life task of a teenager.*

HAIM GINNOTT

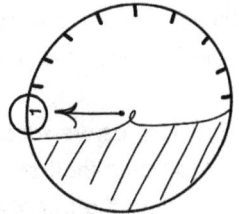

The Driver

The Driver

Many years ago, around the age of twenty-two, a few of my closest friends and I went to visit a friend, receiving support for postnatal depression, at an inner-city hospice. We were invited to attend a group meeting as her support crew.
I distinctly remember feeling depressed, as we sat in a relaxed circle listening to the dressing gown clad patients sharing their stories. The room was drab and the mood expectedly flat, reflecting the lousy weather we had negotiated on route to the hospice.

After awkward introductions and uncomfortable small talk, we were encouraged to assist our friend to brainstorm all her qualities, features, strengths and personality traits. The softly spoken facilitator handed out the obligatory sheets of butcher's paper and a handful of markers, with one strict instruction: we were not to include any restrictive labels of any description; reflecting occupational, marital or family status.

I nominated myself as the scribe and waited for our friend to start throwing ideas at me, reminding myself of the brief to omit words like mother, teacher, dancer, daughter, sister and cousin. I remember as clear as day wondering, *Well, without all of that, who is she?*

When the half hour session came to an end, I looked down to see the butcher's paper full of words like dreamer, ambitious, extrovert, generous and traveler. It was refreshing to think of her in a new way, without the default pattern of restrictive labels.

We could all sense the shift in energy within the room and the new possibilities that lay ahead for our friend. It felt wonderful to be an integral part of her intervention and a catalyst for the redefining and expansiveness of her identity.

As we left her that evening, we vowed to remain her cheer squad for the challenging weeks and months which lay ahead.

Today, whenever I deliver *A Woman's Way* workshops, I ask the women present to explore their identity with the exclusion of titles. Their blank faces take me back to that time so many years ago, where I struggled to formulate my own definition of *Who I Am*.

Ignition Exercise
Who Am I?

Who are you?
I encourage you to jot down some of your qualities, values and strengths that best reflect who you truly are ... remember no labels!
Don't think too much about what sounds right or finding the right words.

Just make note what comes. Try to capture the essence of the real you.

Be real! Who are you?

_____   _____
_____   _____
_____   _____
_____   _____
_____   _____

The Labels We Are Given

I see life as an incredible journey. Along the road, we can be a driver, a passenger, or an onlooker. There are times in life when you can feel like you've got no control or, when times are hard, like you've been 'thrown under the bus'. There are other times when you feel so completely in control that you're the Kombi driver, encouraging others to hop onboard the good life bus.

How confident and capable we feel to drive our own bus and steer our own course can have a lot to do with the labels we have been given in childhood and continue to wear in our adult life.

We come into this world with a name bestowed upon us from our parents. The origin of our name often holds deep significance; honoring grandparents, a beloved aunt or perhaps reflecting the name trends of the time. Regardless, the initial labels we receive are our first and middle names.

As we grow up in our families, we are given new labels in the form of affectionate nicknames; names which reflect our status in the family and our developing personalities. We might be called the favourite, the middle child, chatterbox, daddy's girl, mischief maker, or the quiet one.
At the time we may happily adopt some of these playful labels, but some can be sticky and remain into adulthood, weighing heavily upon us as adults.

At the age of five or six, most of us head off to school where we remain for the next eleven to thirteen years. Labels are handed out like bundles of worksheets, random at times but as permanent as ink.

Developmentally, these years are significant, when our identities are taking shape.

> **Labels are handed out like bundles of worksheets, random at times but as permanent as ink.**

Words and phrases - such as hard worker, class clown, runner, artist, nerd, school captain, high achiever, introvert, artist, gifted, trouble maker, or perfect student - echo through classrooms and are recorded on reports; forever etched in our minds.

Attached to each label are expectations which we might fulfil, surpass or even fail. Some labels we wear proudly, others reluctantly. Consciously or unconsciously, we march on through life wearing these labels like ill-fitting sandwich boards.

The Unwanted Label Of Perfection

Perfectionist was one such label I willingly chose to wear. (If perfectionist was never a badge you wore, you may like to consider one you were given or have adopted yourself, which has restricted your growth or shadowed your identity).

I thought perfectionists were elitists, individuals to be in awe of and inspired by. At school, the perfectionist club, to which I always yearned to belong to, had members who were blessed with perfect physical attributes as well as perfect grades. I had formulated my own childish equation which read something like: beauty + personality = perfection. Perfection leads to popularity, and hence being seen!

How wrong I was. Thankfully, with the gift of hindsight and maturity, I have dismantled and discarded that equation and am content to just be me! I'm pleased to announce that I'm now a recovering perfectionist. It's been nine years, two months and some days since I - awkwardly and somewhat embarrassingly - removed the worn label from my identity.

And, yes, the date is etched clearly and perfectly in my mind.

I was attending a weekend workshop and had summoned up the courage to raise my hand ready to contribute to the conversation. I vaguely recall the facilitator's reaction upon hearing my declaration that I was a perfectionist!

He didn't mince his words, nor stumble over their delivery when he announced that perfectionists have no standards!

Despite my dropped jaw and the growing embarrassment creeping across my face, he continued, attempting to further clarify his statement. It was his belief that perfectionists in general often set themselves unrealistic expectations that soar at incredibly high heights. As a result, those who possess this trait, often find themselves falling short of achieving their specific and highly tuned goals. Close enough is not good enough and simply represents a mediocre compromise for dealing with yet another disappointment.

There it was; the public slap in the face I needed to jolt me from my false sense of identity. That moment tore the label off like the bandaid it had been on my perpetual wound of excuses and justifications.

Ignition Exercise
Identify Your Labels

I encourage you to take a moment to jot down some of the nicknames and labels that you have been given over the years, as well as those that have been self-imposed.

_____   _____
_____   _____
_____   _____
_____   _____

Circle the names or labels that are still used, or still evoke a reaction for you, today!

How do you feel about the names or labels that you have circled?

_____
_____
_____
_____

Cross out the names or labels you dislike/d being called.
Given what you wrote in your first Ignition Exercise 'Who are You?'
How do you feel about these labels? Are any outworn and outdated?

_____
_____
_____

GPS : You Control The Action

As women, we have a reputation for frequently changing our minds.
So, why not live up to that notion and fully embrace the ability to steer yourself in the direction you choose?

We are all driven by our thoughts, dreams, expectations, beliefs, values and emotions. The good news is that like a Kombi driver can override her GPS, so too can you choose a different direction or road to journey upon. Like my favourite children's author, Dr Seuss professes, 'You have brains in your head. You have feet in your shoes. You can steer yourself in any direction you choose.'

As the driver of your Kombi, you truly are gifted with the skills and wisdom to set your own path and blessed with the courage to go forth. Whether you consider the problems you encounter in life as speed bumps, T-intersections or complex roundabouts, they are there to be conquered, and conquer you must. As the driver of your Kombi, your choices shouldn't be limited to bailing out of the Kombi or stopping suddenly on the highway of life's hectic traffic!

We all need to make decisions and sometimes they require instant action, which can be uncomfortable and even painful. Scientists agree that on average, an adult makes approximately 35 000 decisions a day. That's an exhausting thought right there! This abundance of decisions is thrown in with a mix of daily routines of work, family and play. No wonder our beds start summoning us from 7pm each evening.

The Fork In The Road

There are times in life when you either willingly or reluctantly arrive at a fork in the road, which demands a change or choice in direction. These moments are usually inescapable, brought on by predictable circumstances, unfortunate situations or unexpected heartache.

Some women experience many forks in the road throughout their lives, while others seemingly relax into cruise control and flow through life content with the status quo.

Perhaps your own fork in the road has led you to this book. Maybe you have reached rock bottom or have arrived at an intersection demanding a readjustment of your GPS. Honour this moment for the opportunity it is, to consider where you steer your life next.

Whilst forks in the road typically arrive as presents of pain from a deliverer of despair, they often dissolve into gifts of growth.

Life has a wicked sense of humor, which can test us in unimaginable ways. We often feel pulled, pushed and tested by circumstances and challenges. Our strength of character, our attitudes and the intensity of our convictions will determine whether we come out on the other side feeling like we're a victor or victim.

> **Whilst forks in the road typically arrive as presents of pain from a deliverer of despair, they often dissolve into gifts of growth.**

My mother-in-law slipped in her garden pond two years ago. What should have happened next was a series of operations to clean the gaping wound and locate and secure stray bones. The reality was a nightmarish tapestry of loosely woven stitches and skin grafts sewn into her lifeless leg. As her family, we became the helpless bystanders, bemused by the train wreck of medical excuses, blunders and gross incompetence. Seven months after the fall, my mother-in-law's desperate pleas were finally heard. Her left leg was amputated just below the knee, revealing stage two of her living hell.

Over the years that followed, I never once attended or heard of any self-pity parties hosted by my mother-in-law. Her grit, doggedness and determination were beacons of hope for us. With every milestone, regardless of the enormity of the challenge, came simple celebrations in her matter-of-fact way.
I truly believe that her fierce and unwavering attitude became her much needed best friend in the darkest of days and nights. Her independent steps were few, but her determination continued to astound us.

She proved that the victim/victor mentality is purely choice driven. She relentlessly faced daily and hourly challenges and I'm sure just even getting out of bed conjured up dark thoughts and a reluctancy to go on another day.

My mother-in-law was a fighter; for she didn't know any other way.
Courage and independence were the faithful crutches upon which her life quite literally depended. As the driver of your own Kombi I encourage you to be constantly victorious, the owner of your choices, the master of your actions. Seize each moment with unwavering courage and be curious.
Don't just ask the usual victim questions: Why me? Why now? What now?
Why not rephrase your questions and ask Why NOT me? Why NOT now?
Get curious and ask the bigger questions: Who can I become through this? What can I do to take the next step?

Be alert and aware of the abundance of options that surround you.
When you choose to shift into gear and make your next move, you'll be amazed at how many roads open up for you.
The action/s you take next will either strengthen your identity or suppress your power; shift you up a gear or out of gear.
Your fork in the road is an opportunity to clearly discover your true self.
Be a victor of circumstance; a victor who can and will conquer all she faces!

<u>My Big Fat Fork In The Road</u>

I watched the demonstration like a schoolgirl hanging off her teacher's every word. Dutifully curious, inwardly I was preparing to embrace the unknown. For years, I had the limiting belief that to be heard, you needed to be loud! Loud voices, loud gestures, loud opinions! I had struggled with this concept for most of my adult life. I was always quiet; quietly spoken, quietly focused, quietly achieving, quietly respectful, yet quietly unnoticed!

And then with words unspoken, I got it!

It happened in a dusty horse arena, far from my home, on a property in San Jose, California. My dearest friend Gaynor and I had travelled from Cochrane, Alberta, Canada on a whim to meet with a horse whisperer, Diane.

We watched Diane lead, send off and join up with her mare with silent expertise. Not a single verbal instruction passed her lips. Our agenda was simple: watch, learn and copy.
I naively believed I could fulfil that agenda, no problems! I had been quietly watching, learning and copying since childhood. I was what you would call a model student. Just don't ask me to read aloud, answer any questions or have an opinion. Both my parents had reinforced the importance of being seen and not heard, being polite and not loud. I called their words of wisdom, The Golden Rules.
If you followed The Golden Rules, then you would be liked and become a somebody. The problem was that I was the most polite and well-mannered child I knew but I felt like a nobody. I remained loyal to The Golden Rules until I stepped into that arena in October 2010.

After watching Diane's demonstration and powered by an unknown source of confidence and adrenalin, I stood to my feet, swallowed my nerves and volunteered to go first. I tentatively made my way down the dry patched hill towards the arena. My mare waited and nuzzled in closer to Diane as I approached. I felt and admired their connection and was sure I heard her whisper in its ear, "Be kind with this one."

"I've given you a quiet horse," Diane casually mentioned.

Hmm, because that's all you can handle, retorted a cruel voice within. And there it was, the cutting voice of my ego. I pushed its unwanted words to a place where it wouldn't hurt me. This was my time to shine.

With the exception of a disinterested stocky mare, I stood alone and vulnerable; I felt stripped of my beloved 'mask' - a mask which hid my true self and had become so easy to wear and natural to hide behind. To be blunt, I was experiencing the highest peak of anxiousness.

Whilst the verbal instructions had been few, the intention was crystal clear. Diane's words reverberated through my body, lost yet begging to be found.

> *Lead, don't follow.*
> *Energy up.*
> *Disguise your fear.*
> *Own your presence.*
> *Channel your inner strength.*
> *Pause. Carry on. Pause. Turn. Pause.*

In the silent arena, I had to lift my energy to a level which would motivate my mare to canter around the fence line, unattached to me. Once in a natural and comfortable stride, she would await my cue to slow to a trot and then if I was successful, she would rejoin me in the centre of the arena.

The first 15 minutes were torturous as all my insecurities assembled deep in my heart and disgorged from my body. I had nowhere to hide.
My discomfort and embarrassment swelled in the pockets of my eyes and I blinked with growing intensity. I tried desperately to suppress the bulging dam wells on the verge of bursting under the weight of my mortification.
Like a child, I sought connection and possibly instruction from Diane who stood silently outside of the arena.
She offered me nothing. This was my battle; a raging war requiring sole intervention. I could wave my white flag and surrender to its power or rise with its force. And rise I did!

In the hours of equine interaction that followed that day, the powerful insight I gained was enlightening! No human words or touch had ever managed to bring me to this point. It had taken the powerful presence and energy of a horse to finally capture and release my quietly suppressed strength - I found my inner voice!

My interaction with the mare required no words, no touch. It relied purely on self love, self motivation, self confidence and self surrender - all summoned from within!

We built mutual trust and respect with words unspoken. As the day drew to an end, I stood in front of two very special friends and made a pledge. I made a vow to honor my soul, my heart and my mind by being true to myself and to speak only words of truth, of kindness and of inspiration.

This was the day I discovered the true meaning of my authentic self.
I vowed to be replace thoughts and words of self judgement and self pity, with encouragement and empowerment.

From that point on, that fork in the road arena moment, I shattered a handful of distorted and limiting beliefs that had shaped my identity for so long.
I realised that being an introvert meant strength in silence in a noisy world.
I walked away with quiet confidence, aware of the newly found promise I had made with myself. I had reconnected with the real me and left the ego driven self, by the roadside.

In the chaos I found peace, in my discomfort I found ease.

Your Fork In The Road

A fork in the road moment can and will change your life. It will shake things up and provide you with invaluable hindsight and insight. It will redefine you and prepare you for the successive challenges which will no doubt follow.
The greatest gift of a fork in the road is the rush you will experience as you hurtle through its forces. A mirror of self reflection will be held in front of you, forcing you to examine your values, your strengths and your challenges.

As you travel through the tunnels of darkness and weave through the chicanes of options, you will steer towards your authentic self. You will emerge from the darkness to reveal the real you and the woman the world is waiting to meet!
You are the driver of your Kombi and your driver seat awaits!

Ignition Exercise
Your Fork In the Road Moment

Set the timer for 15-20 minutes and reflect upon and record a memorable fork in the road moment which impacted you in a way that redefined you and helped in shaping your identity.

_____
_____
_____
_____
_____
_____
_____
_____
_____
_____
_____
_____
_____
_____
_____
_____
_____
_____
_____
_____

We are all branded with names, titles and roles, that's a given! However, the only expectations we have to live up to are the ones that we place on ourselves. As Phillip McGraw says in his book, *Self Matters*, 'Labels are generalisations or stereotypes that ignore who we truly are.'

Whether it's self imposed or someone else's perception of you, labels are eligible for review at any point. Just like in the good old days when we renewed our vehicle registration with a new sticker, we can adjust our labels tto change the direction of our lives based on the decisions we make.
Luckily, we don't have to wait for annual vehicle registration renewals, we can review and update every minute and every hour of every day.

Fork in the Road moments are our heart and soul's way of begging for change out of a deep need to find joy, fulfillment and empowerment. Be prepared to be vulnerable and brace for uncertainty, but no matter what, enjoy the journey and the incredible woman that you are becoming!

Ignition Exercise

Your Journey So Far

What have you discovered about yourself so far in these pages that make you feel better prepared for your journey ahead?

_____
_____
_____
_____
_____
_____
_____
_____
_____
_____
_____
_____
_____
_____
_____

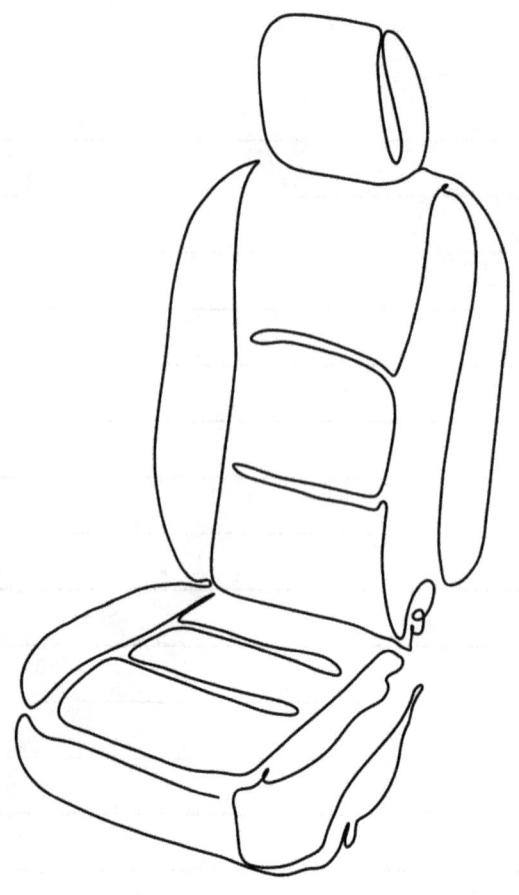

*Values are like fingerprints.
Nobody's are the same,
but you leave them all over everything you do.*

ELVIS PRESLEY

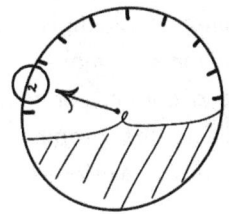

The Driver's Seat

The Driver's Seat

One of the fondest memories I have of time spent with my father, was sitting on his lap in the driver's seat of his 1982 Chrysler Sigma sedan. It was only ever reserved for the weekends on the rural property our friends owned, outside of Marulan in the Southern Tablelands of New South Wales. The 100 acre sprawling property was home to mobs of curious kangaroos and just beyond the farm gates, stood a quaint, yet comfortable makeshift dwelling. We loved our weekend visits to the property and always saw it as an opportunity to escape our suburban existence and slip into relaxed country living.

My driving lessons with my father would normally take place in the early afternoons when the adults were chilled and us kids were restless and in search of some entertainment. My father would throw me an all too familiar grin, escaping beneath his neatly groomed beard. He would flare his nose out repeatedly and raise a cheeky eyebrow at his set of car keys, which lay in wait upon the glass topped coffee table.

This routine was comfortably predictable and ours to enjoy. Looking back, I'm unsure if my conservative and safety conscious mother approved, but there never seemed to be any dark clouds of disapproval. To be honest, I think she was happy to sink into the afternoon's sunshine, sipping on shandies and engaging in idle conversation with her friends.

Left to do the steering, whilst my dad managed the accelerator and brakes, I would always giggle with delight.
I loved him for trusting me to safely guide our family car around the paddock, despite being way too young to have a driver's licence! I never felt nervous as I sat perched high upon his lap. I was my daddy's girl and he treated me like a princess, a queen in waiting.

I felt 10 foot tall and in control; a wonderful experience for a twelve year old girl who spent most of her time hovering awkwardly over the threshold of uncertainty and wavering self-esteem.

He would often feign panic and insist that I take full control, to which I would tilt my head out of the open window and squeal with delight. The summers spent driving with my father were magical and I treasured our time together. He never instructed me as such or corrected my immature steering. Instead, he seemed to share in my excitement as my courage grew and I took safe risks under his watchful eye.

Now, as I reflect on that precious time with my dad, it reinforces so many wonderful realisations. The woman I am today, and the child I was then, are strongly influenced by my parents' values, beliefs, and the nurturing environment they nested me in. Fearlessness is one of my father's core values. He is fearless of change and adventure.

When he fearlessly let me drive upon his lap, I felt fearless! To this day, I remain cautiously adventurous, if that's even a thing! Whilst I'm no adrenalin seeking, adventure devotee, I am adventurous in the sense that I'm ready and willing to step way beyond my comfort zone.

What Is The Value Of Values

Values are the personal beliefs which guide us and motivate our actions and attitudes. They help determine what is important to us and what is worth nurturing, chasing and discarding. Our values describe the personal qualities we embrace and those we embody. They paint a picture of who we want to be and how we want to be treated.

Values are like magnets which point our compass in the direction of our preferred journey. Having strong faith in your values will illuminate the highway of your life and help you find meaning and purpose.

I truly believe that our identity is formed by the foundation of our actions, which reflect our values. In contrast, when your actions are erratic and out of character, chances are you are out of alignment with your authentic self.

In his book, *Unapologetically You*, Steve Maraboli suggests that a lot of the conflict that we have in our lives exists because we're not being true to ourselves. So how do we align our values with our true self?

Ignition Exercise
Explore Your Values

Values reflect what is important to us. So, ask yourself "What is important to me?"
Is it family, connection, success, health, fitness, career, mastery, adventure, community, travel, kindness, loyalty, career, security?

_____   _____
_____   _____
_____   _____
_____   _____
_____   _____

What warms your heart? What sparks joy?

What drives you crazy and keeps you awake at night?

Chances are your responses will provide you with some indication of your values. Also, reflect on your journaled thoughts from Chapter 1, when you were identifying personality traits and qualities in your identity work.

Acceptance	Love	Beauty	Joy	Wisdom
Connection	Responsibility	Family	Creativity	Justice
Significance	Discipline	Grace	Balance	Passion
Respect	Motivation	Honour	Variety	Knowledge
Curiosity	Trust	Risk	Teamwork	Patience
Service	Independence	Talent	Warmth	Leadership
Adventure	Fairness	Community	Kindness	Gratitude
Equality	Friendship	Faith	Courage	Fun
Skill	Authenticity	Commitment	Harmony	Unity
Spirituality	Happiness	Security	Vision	Health

Consider the table above as a collection of values. Take some time to choose from the table - or from your own self-knowledge - four to six values that you hold dear. Be specific and include only the values that embrace, support, protect and cradle you. After all, this chapter is about choosing the best fitting driver's seat for your journey.

_____
_____
_____
_____
_____
_____

Values help define how we want to live. So, ask yourself, how do I want to live?

In responding to this question, focus on the HOW you want to live instead of the *where* you live or want to live.

While my physical home (where I live) is an 18 acre property south west of Sydney, *how* I choose to live is all about creating a simple yet full life.
My husband, Adam and I share our simplistic, yet wholesome existence with our two adult children, Isabelle and Isaac. This is the only home that they have known, and they're both adamant it must remain in our family.

When we first looked at the house, (pre children), we instantly knew it would be a wonderful playground for making treasured memories. Our property is now home to five chickens (Miss Mustard, Blanco, Little Hen, Trixie and Dixie), two dogs (Apollo and Athena), and a three-year-old cow, named Lucy Moo.
Simplicity is the river that runs through our lives. Isabelle (Belle) and Isaac have only ever known tank water; a sacred water supply shared with thriving tree frogs. The air is simply fresh, my garden is a simple palette of colour and beauty and I have had mixed results with seasonal vegetables and herbs.
I'm a barefoot gardener and love to feel the freshly turned soil between my toes. I feel obliged to apologise to foot masseurs for the state of my cracked heels, on the odd occasion when I indulge in a massage.

Our home can be best described as a unique treehouse. We live in a pole home, designed and built solely around telegraph poles, sunk approximately four metres underground. My interior decorating palette is simple yet functional; adventurous yet earthy.

My goal is to live a minimalistic life, with each furnishing holding an interesting story or anecdote. The artworks which adorn our walls are all lovingly created by my children and myself.
To honour the memory of the famous comedian and actor, Robin Williams, I painted a sizeable portrait which hangs proudly in my lounge room.

It's by no means perfect, but the imperfections are swallowed by his infectious smile and expressive eyes. The portrait breathes life and light into our home and always makes me smile.

My core value of simplicity defines how and where I choose to live.
I could and would live anywhere, as long as it was with simplicity. During the devastating bushfire season that haunted our shire in January 2020, we had each packed a washing basket with our most treasured belongings and stored them away safely in our shipping container. If asked now to recall the items within my basket, I could name them without too much thought. To me, that's what simple living is about and what keeps me grounded and focused on how I want to live my life.

Ignition Exercise
How Do You Want To Live?

Sometimes asking yourself the question, *how do I want to live?* provides you with the clarity you crave in identifying your values.

So, how do you want to live? _____
_____
_____
_____
_____
_____

Living By Your Values

I'm sure my daughter Belle entered this world already thirsty for knowledge and blessed with the curiosity of a cat. This blessing remained a faithful companion throughout her formal years of education. I lost track of the number of awards she received and the assemblies that I attended.
On paper, she read like a finely tuned Kombi destined for an amazing life journey, with the built-in sustainability to complete life's most grueling challenges.

However, months before her HSC, her fuel tank ran dry and her spark plugs failed to ignite. She issued a personal defect notice that read: *I no longer comply with the high standards expected predominantly by myself and of others. I hereby deem myself defective and incapable of operating in an acceptable manner.*

Just like that, she gave herself permission to rip the constricting labels from the identity that others had manufactured. The highly strung, walking library that my daughter had become, fell apart. The timing couldn't have been worse, but is there ever a perfect time to pull into the breakdown lane?

True to form, Belle listened to her intuition, the one remaining certainty in her life. Like a well-oiled engine built on trust and honesty, she followed her heart. She politely turned her back on her university placement offers, enrolled in TAFE and completed her certification in Learning Support.
She wanted to draw on her own love of learning, and inspire children who had also lost their way or had become distracted.

Belle challenged herself and the expectations of others and dived deeply into her vault of values. I'm so proud of her ability to muster the courage to roll the dice of opportunity at such a young age and live strongly by her decisions.

All too often, we find ourselves either attempting to live up to the expectations of others or trying in vain to mimic the lives of those who we think we admire. How exhausting! How inauthentic! Life poses a multitude of choices for us, disguised in the form of intersections, traffic lights, roundabouts, fork in the road moments and even detours.

By fine tuning our personal GPS systems - our values - we can approach our choices with the strength and blessing of deep intuition and the clarity of self assurance. That feels like open road freedom to me; owning my choices and following them freely!

Choose Your Seat, Chose Your Values

Values are imposed by our family and upbringing throughout childhood, developed and reinforced during adolescence and then road tested throughout adulthood. The good news is that as adults we get the opportunity to reconsider, redefine and realign our values with our identity and lifestyle.
As a woman you have the ability, through your voice and actions, to change your values if they no longer nurture, support, challenge or serve you. If this sounds like something you need now, open your heart to the possibility of discovering a new 'seat' of values that may feel tight at first but, when you relax into them, feel like you're home.
When delivering my workshops based on the teachings in this book, I often ask participants to engage in a fun, simple and highly effective exercise. Using a chair, I ask them to write down one of their core values and place it on the seat. I then ask them to write on post it notes, four ways that they are currently living by this value.

For example, a woman who has chosen kindness as her core value may write the following statements to affirm that her value of kindness is in alignment with her identity:

1. I speak with inner kindness to myself.
2. I compliment random strangers who have made me feel joy.
3. I speak with reassurance and kindness to the children I teach.
4. I become physically emotional when I witness acts of kindness.

This exercise helps to think about your values and what they can look like in everyday action. These four ways on post-it-notes represent the four legs of the chair; how they 'sit in' and are supported by their value.

My father is going straight to heaven when he passes. He could quite easily be the kindest human being I know. He would do anything for anyone, at any time. He models kindness so effortlessly that its contagious force must have permeated my soul as a child and has become one of my deepest and dearest values.

However, our beliefs, opinions and values will sometimes differ from our peers, our colleagues, our partners and at times, our family. I believe that the binding connection that our values share, is the wholesome intention of bringing goodness to life.

So, when choosing your values be mindful of hand selecting ones that fit you well and not the image of you; the one you're trying to uphold. Be free of judgement of the values others choose to live by, remember that they too are doing the best they can with the values and resources available to them.

When you free yourself from the judgement of others you are relinquishing your own concern about their opinions of you and your values.

Whilst completing my Certificate 4 in Life Coaching, I came across the powerful leadership model; the Be-Do-Have model. I love the simplicity of this model. The key message is: Who do I need to *Be* to do what I need to *Do* in order to have what I want to *Have*?

The Be refers to your values, the Do is your actions and the Have will be your destination. Simple really! Unless we support the Be (our values) with what we Do (our actions) then we won't have what we seek (our results). We can take baby steps or giant leaps, as long as we engage in some form of action.

I recently had a revelation about the phrase human being. I prefer my new take on the phrase - human becoming.

> ❝ **I recently had a revelation about the phrase human being. I prefer my new take on the phrase - human becoming.** ❞

While both words contain the word BE, to me, the word becoming conjures up the idea of a work in progress rather than being, which assumes the destination has been reached!

Here's an example of what a Be-Do-Have statement could look like:

To be _____ authentic _____
(BE/VALUE)

I need to _____ speak my truth and put my needs first _____
(DO/ACTION)

so that I will have a peaceful mind knowing that I have been authentic
(HAVE/RESULT)

Ignition Exercise
The Be-Do-Have Model

Now it's your turn. Take a moment to complete this affirmation.

To be _____(VALUE)
I need to _____(ACTION)
so that I will have _____(RESULT)

Now try another affirmation

To be _____ (VALUE)

I need to _____ (ACTION)

so that I will have _____ (RESULT)

<u>Customise Your Seat, Customise Your Values</u>

When you customise your driver's seat to suit your personal comfort, you are in essence aligning your actions with your values. Like any driver's seat, it should have a few key features to ensure your comfort, safety and enjoyment.

Relax into your seat of values, live by them, live in them and for them. That is how and where you will find your strength and your purpose and enjoy reaching your destination. You will experience the joy of being in control rather than the feeling of being controlled and driven by someone else's values.

Once you are clear on your identity and the values that support you, you are almost ready to embark on your journey. This is not to say there is anything wrong with sitting in discomfort (or a slightly uncomfortable seat) for a period of time whilst choosing your values. We've all driven life this way at some point. Your value journey is personal and requires dedicated reflection.

Be ruthless if required! Or sit in silence, if necessary. You are your best friend and because of this, you know which is the most effective method to spring cleaning your values and your life.

Have you ever heard people admit, when heading off on a holiday, that they are on a journey of discovery to find themselves? Don't get me wrong, travel is a great way or excuse to find the real you, but you can also do that from the comfort of your own home. When you or someone you know is 'finding themselves', perhaps they're trying to find new values.

One of my all-time favourite quotes by Shakespeare is: 'Wherever you go, there you are!' My interpretation of that is, that you may travel all you like, drive as far as you can, or hide for as long as possible, but you still won't shake the who that you are - the perfectly imperfect woman seeking to be seen heard and loved!

Your Number Plate

Upon getting his Ps (provisional licence) at 17, my son was able to purchase customised number plates for a significant fee. Whilst it is beyond me to understand why he feels compelled to commit to such a financial burden, I reminded myself that it is not my endeavour to endure. However, I will use it as an example for this chapter.

My son takes great pride in his car, and rightly so. On the cusp of turning 20, he owns two cars in a growing fleet of his beloved brand. One of his core values is perseverance, and although it can often be the bane of my existence, I love and admire the fire in his belly that drives and motivates his actions.

During his senior school years, if I wasn't replying to a steady stream of emails from his teachers imploring him to commit more to his studies, then I would be gently reminding him that all good things come to those who wait. I have no doubt that my son will one day boast of his executive role in the prestigious car company that he has set his heart and eyes on since the age of ten.

My son encompasses the word unique to a T. Unfortunately for his teachers, but fortunately for the world post school, he is our square peg in a world filled with round holes. Luckily, most square pegs have incredible vision, astute awareness of their gifts and the conviction to stamp their mark on this world. His personalised number plates reveal not only his name but also his identity as a driven and unique young man.

Ignition Exercise

Your Personalised Number Plate

If you could choose one value that means more than anything to you and use it as your number plate, what would it read?

```
┌─────────────────────────────┐
│                             │
│                             │
└─────────────────────────────┘
```

Values are what drives our decisions and steers us in a direction that feels authentic and true. They reflect what we consider important in making our lives wonderful and worthwhile. We use our values to deliberately focus our time and energy on what is important to us.

As we have discovered in this chapter, our values are strongly influenced and formed according to our family's beliefs, our personal life experiences and the environment we choose to settle into.

Our identity is defined by our values and they in turn influence our actions. Now, armed with clarity around your identity and your values, the next step of your journey awaits.

Let's make the windscreen of your goals and dreams clean, clear and ready to reveal your path! Dream big and go forth with courage and curiosity!

Trip notes

Hold the vision, trust the process.

UNKNOWN

The Windscreen

The Windscreen

I have always wanted to write my own book. I have dabbled in a few halfhearted attempts, but my first real taste of being a published author was as an excited eleven-year-old. My mind was swimming with ideas. I remember relishing in the writing task set by my Year 6 teacher. I have no recollection of the content of the narrative I wrote but I distinctively recall the neatly typed pages that my mother helped me produce and the personally decorated cardboard folder which housed my work.

The feedback I was given from my teacher was average but fortunately, not disheartening enough to dampen my spirits and passion for writing. I have always loved writing and at last count, I am proud to say I'm the owner of twelve treasured journals that I have kept since my first, at the age of nine. Most are personal journals, with the inclusion of a few travel and baby memoirs, all neatly packed into a beautifully crafted floral hatbox. As I travelled through my early twenties and into my mid 40's, I would eagerly count down to the final strike of midnight to announce my New Year's resolutions.

Sure enough, each loose promise held the space for one simple wish - keep a journal. I would stay driven and committed for three to five months and then the distraction of life provided an exit ramp! I'm not sure why I never sustained a regular journal writing practice; the important thing for me was that I started, and the journals remain available if my children or grandchildren ever seek deeper insight into my life!

Armed with the greatest of intentions, I always seemed to fall short in my commitment to achieving my writing goals. Well, that was until a month before I started work on this book, when I came across an advertisement on my Instagram feed. In true social media form, the ad appeared in response to my increasing interest in self-publishing in 2020.

As fortune has it, a writing coach by the name of Emma Franklin Bell became the lifebuoy in my sea of overwhelm. She was offering a five day online writing challenge and I felt that this was my sign from the universe. From there I committed to her four to five month writing process.

I could tell you it was an easy ride to achieve my goal of writing my book, but that would be completely untrue. With strict adherence to specifically structured steps, I inched closer and closer to the realisation of my long-awaited goal of self-publishing my own book.

I am a systems kind of girl and I thrive when tasks are simple, straight forward and reflect my values. I approached each face-to-face call and written task with the excitement and curiosity of a child. I was in my element and certain that the armour of confidence which embraced me, would sustain this new writing commitment and see me through to the end. And it did!

Preparing The Windscreen

We are travelling on this road of self discovery by way of a Kombi. The windscreen plays a crucial part in this journey because it shows us where we're heading.

We can look out through the expanse of the clear windscreen and see the direction of our dreams – our vision. We can see from this vantage point that our goals and dreams are in the distance in front of us, and there are things we must do as we ride along to ensure we drive towards them.

Goals & Systems

What is a goal?
You're no doubt familiar with the term *goal*; a desired result that a person initiates, plans and commits to achieve. Goals can be outcome, process or performance based.

Goals which are *outcomes based* refer to the desired end result - your destination.
Performance based goals identify specific standards to be achieved - your itinerary.
Whereas *process based* goals, deal with the techniques necessary to perform well - your driving skills.
For now, we'll focus on destination goals, those we can see in the distance through our windscreen. Most people have goals for different aspects of their life: personal, business, life, health, family, wealth. Goals are *what* we want to achieve, the vision we see through our windscreen of life.

<u>What Is A System?</u>

A system is a set of action steps you need to take to achieve your goal. Systems are the processes you follow on a regular basis to bring you closer to your goal. Think of the system as your gear box. The goal is your destination, where you are heading, and the system is the gearbox you'll use to shift gears to pick up speed and move forward along your journey.

If you want to reach your destination within a set timeframe, it's important to have strong systems in place. The most powerful systems are:
- specific
- flexible
- enjoyable
- in alignment with your values
- given the priority they richly deserve

Here are some examples to illustrate my point.

GOAL: Lose weight!
SYSTEM: Walk for 30 minutes each day, enjoy smaller servings, speak with a dietician or nutritionist, join a gym, keep a food journal.

GOAL: Be calmer!
SYSTEM: Download a meditation app, meditate each morning before breakfast, keep a gratitude journal, enrol in yoga classes.

GOAL: Write a book!
SYSTEMS: Buy a journal, connect with an author/mentor and seek advice on where to start, sign up for a writing course, create a writing space.

Ignition Exercise
Create Your Gear Box Systems

Have a go at writing some of your own examples, remembering to:
1. Choose a simple and practical goal that is achievable for you and write that down.

2. Think about the simplest steps you could take to achieve that goal. Remember that these steps (or gear changes) form the system to achieve the goal.

3. Write down those steps in order and they will create the system.

GOAL_____

SYSTEM

1. _____
2. _____
3. _____

GOAL _____
_____

SYSTEM

1. _____
2. _____
3. _____

I could have manifested the most vivid vision of my completed book - like a projection of what I wanted to happen - but without the systems (gear change steps), I would just get caught up in the romanticism of the vision. You may sit in front of the cleanest windscreen, with the clearest vision, but you'll go nowhere unless you shift into gear to use the power of the engine, wheels and whole vehicle to gain momentum.

Goals are important in setting direction, but systems create the traction to get you moving! Every car comes with an operation manual; a set of detailed systems on how to drive your car. Yes, we can successfully drive from point A to B without referring to the manual, but in times of trouble, the car manual is within easy access and contains detailed and specific systems for you to activate.

A Woman's Way is your manual, your personalised operational manual for the journey ahead!

Ignition Exercise
What Brought You On This Journey?

I'm curious. What brought you to this book? Was it a recommendation, a connection, an instinct or fate?
When you picked up *A Woman's Way* what did you hope to get out of reading it?

_____

_____

Whatever your reason, I'm so glad that you are here and embarking on this adventure. I know that windscreens can get dirty and obstruct your vision. Whatever stage you feel you're up to in your journey, we're on this trip of consciousness together, and I'll help clean the windscreen for you while you steer.

Perhaps you have reached a crossroad on your journey. You may have arrived at what Dr Seuss calls *the waiting place*! It's a place where people are waiting to make decisions and waiting to take action; a place where you seek inspiration, encouragement and validation about your next step.

Think of all these waiting places as rest areas on your journey.
Maybe, you have heard a faint whisper within which has grown deeper in its urgency. Steven Spielberg echoes these words when he says: 'Your human, personal intuition always whispers, it never shouts. It's very hard to hear.
So you have to, every day of your life, be ready to hear what whispers in your ear.'

For me, I had reached a point in my teaching career where 20 years of gathered wisdom and experience could no longer sustain my happiness or bring me joy. My engine had stopped working and my outdated operational manual was no longer relevant. Teaching had been a dutiful servant, offering me both challenges and success along the way. I had forged the most incredible connections with students and their families and witnessed the positive impacts on young, impressionable minds.

Like a grueling training session that had lasted too long, I was exhausted from teaching. The mounting paperwork, accountability requirements, political correctness and inconsistent support from executives all attributed to my burnout. I was completely clear about what I *didn't* want to do any longer; I just had to work out what I *did* want! I had to devise a new and personalised operational manual!

Throughout the days and weeks ahead, uncertainty grew heavy and weighed me down. The one and only thing that remained true was I wanted to empower children through my work. I knew in my heart my goal was clear, but the teaching environment had to change. So, I made a loose plan which involved following simple steps, away from my classroom door.

If you're feeling you're at this point – lost and in need of a new operation manual – don't despair.

I know from experience that in order to be truly found, you first have to be lost, sometimes completely lost.

Below are a collection of powerful questions I asked myself to create a new operation manual in line with my goals. It'll help you create a clearer vision, so you can observe your options and get back on the road again with confidence and heart.

Ignition Exercise
Your New Operation Manual

Wrap yourself in a cloak of childlike curiosity as you pose and ponder the important questions below and watch the answers play out across your page.

Think carefully and honestly about your responses, for they will lead you towards the development of simple, practical and effective systems – your new operational manual!

It is important to identify where you are heading. Dig deep and identify the heartspace that you want to live in. It's easy to succumb to the sheep mentality, blindly following the status quo. Similarly, be aware if you are unconsciously relying on a generic GPS to map out your path and ultimately your destination.

Where am I heading or want to be heading? _____
_____
_____

In which areas of my life am I living according to others' expectations of what is best for me?
_____
_____
_____

In which areas of my life am I on autopilot?
_____
_____
_____

In which areas of my life am I in the hot seat, raring to kick start my journey?

_____
_____
_____

Why is *Where am I heading or want to be heading* important to me?

_____
_____
_____
_____
_____

How will I get there? Which steps (gear change systems) do I need to follow regularly that will move me closer to my destination?

_____
_____
_____
_____
_____

Am I achieving the results I want? If not, what changes can I make?

_____
_____
_____
_____

By regularly checking in with the progress of your actions, you will be able to modify and redefine your systems, whilst your goal remains the same.

DASHBOARD WARNING! The questions above may create branches of further questions, so be prepared to journey deeper, to gain clarity. My responses below may act as a guide for you. They were written prior to my commitment to writing this book.

1. Where am I heading?
I would like to write and publish my own self empowerment book.

2. How will I get there?
I will write every day for a month.

3. Am I achieving the results I want?
Not really, as there are always distractions like dinner preparation, grocery shopping and various appointments to keep. By the end of the day, I fall asleep in my armchair, pencil poised in my hand, nothing written.

4. So, what changes can I make?
I can create a specific writing space, start a morning writing routine before work, register for an online writing workshop.

As a teacher, I have always believed that the journey is more important than the destination. So much so, that this belief formed the foundation of my philosophy on teaching and learning. As growth and curiosity are two of my core values, it would be amiss of me to not apply a similar philosophy when writing this book.

I have followed specific systems with the vigilance of an airline pilot, expertly commanding her aircraft through the skies to its destination.
I encourage you to be mindful of your journey as opposed to fixated on your destination. Celebrate the small steps, applaud your bravery and adventurous spirit.

Remember, that often it's our impatience for results which distorts our growth, depletes our enthusiasm and dulls the joy of success. Keep your destination clear through your windscreen on the horizon and rely on your peripheral vision to hold your gaze and keep the journey joyous and spontaneous.

Actions Speak Louder Than Words

'Actions speak louder than words': the powerful words once spoken by Abraham Lincoln. I'm optimistic that most of us agree; in order to achieve a goal we must take action.

Let's take a look at what happens if we avoid taking action and how this impacts us long term. There are always short cuts to explore in life, but I wonder how many lead us to where we truly wanted to go? If you find yourself a little lacking in motivation, consider the cost of inaction! Ask yourself, If I avoid this action, what will my life look like in three weeks, three months, three years. Perhaps the thought of what you *won't* have may be the catalyst you need to ignite and initiate action.

Author and motivational speaker, Jim Rohn believes that we must all suffer from one of two pains; the pain of discipline or the pain of regret.

The Ignition Exercise below will allow you to explore this concept.

Ignition Exercise
Pain Of Procrastination

Take a moment to complete the phrase/s below. If you are a chronic procrastinator, I challenge you to complete more than one phrase.

Example
If I avoid going to the gym, then I will feel disappointed in myself and I will be wasting my gym membership fees and I will feel lousy.

If I avoid _____ then _____
_____
_____

If I avoid _____ then _____
_____
_____

If I avoid _____ then _____
_____
_____

Procrastination is the thief of one's time and leads to habitual patterns of guilt and excuses. If this rings true for you, here are some top tips.

- Create To Do lists with small, specific tasks.
- Set time frames for specific tasks.
- Minimise digital distractions whilst completing tasks.
- Reward yourself! This creates a win-win situation; you'll enjoy the fruits of your labour and are more likely to stay motivated.
- Finding the right accountability buddy means that your usual reel of excuses will most likely fall on deaf ears.

Of course, as with any advice you're given, you need to adapt the suggestions to suit your personality type. You know the challenges you face when it comes to completing tasks so be kind, yet firm, and remember - make a small step a big priority!

❝ **Procrastination is the thief of one's time and leads to habitual patterns of guilt and excuses.** ❞

Blurred Vision

Goals are often as quick to be disbanded as they are to be devised. What was once clear in your windscreen can become blurred. There are several reasons why this can occur:

* Procrastination
* Distractions
* Fear of failure
* Boredom or disinterest
* Misalignment with values &/or self
* Time restraints
* Feelings of overwhelm
* No starting point
* Financial limitations

A racing car driver may spend the entire race staring at the leaderboard (the goal) all she likes, but unless she has completed fitness training, accelerates and brakes during the race and focuses on the track with a positive mindset, it's pointless.

Utilising your peripheral vision to check in along the way, rather than the tunnel vision of your goals, will ensure a far more enjoyable and rewarding journey. These factors aside, if you have hit a pothole which has stopped you in your tracks or veered you off course, consider if you have been focusing on the goal rather than the systems.

Heart-Head-Hands Model

I am a dreamer and I'll shout it from the rooftops. I always have been and always will be. I have the ability to while away many hours dreaming visual thoughts or written prose. It's the freedom of thoughts and the ease in which they flow that I love. Dreamers have visions as well as goals. However, in my case, I'm often the helium balloon in need of a weight to keep me grounded. By grounded, I mean able to maintain a balance between having my head in the clouds and my feet on the ground to travel my journey.

Walt Disney, film producer and innovator, utilised a brilliantly simple way of identifying and realising amazing visions. This involved the refinement of brainstormed ideas through the movement of three phases; the dreamer, the realist and the critic stages. To personalise the process for you, I have developed and adopted my own names for each stage.

The Heart Stage

The Heart stage is dedicated to the free flow of fantasies, ideas and possibilities. This step is rich in its organic rawness and my favourite step to explore. I urge you to take your time with this exercise and create a beautiful space which will ignite the playground of your creativity.

Create an ambience which is cosy and free from distractions. Play music, light candles, sip from your favourite cup - you get the gist! Prepare to unleash! Dream big. Don't sweat the small stuff. Anything goes in this phase.

Ignition Exercise
Heart-Head-Hands

For 5-10 minutes (longer if you wish), jot down every goal, dream, wish, idea you have ever imagined. With heightened awareness record any thought that presents itself, regardless of its absurdity. Let your thoughts flow, let them swim to the surface and scoop them up.

_____
_____
_____
_____
_____
_____
_____
_____
_____
_____
_____
_____

The Head Stage

The Head stage is where the dreams that you poured out above, are addressed. Each idea needs to be considered for its practicality and achievability.

During this phase, ideas need to be simplified, clarified and redefined in order to become possibilities. In some cases, adjustments will need to be made.

Now, find a space (preferably different to your HEART space) where you are free from distractions and interruptions. Devise a formula for how best to identify the *keepers*, the *maybes* and the *not likelys*, from your pool of brainstormed ideas.

Highlighters are great here - or columns - to put into categories. The choice is yours, so get creative! A little tip: Perhaps highlight the dreams that scream for your attention (keeper); circle the dreams that are quietly waving (maybe) and strike out those that don't conjure strong connections (not likely).

DASHBOARD WARNING! There is the strong possibility that you could plummet into overwhelm here, so be prepared. If the ego steps in to play devil's advocate and casts shadows over your dreams, dig deeper in your resolve to persevere or revisit this exercise when you have a clear head. Be kind to yourself. This exercise is an integral step towards creating your vision.

<u>The Hand Stage</u>

The Hand stage is the action phase, the roll up the sleeves and get messy step. This is the weight to my balloon, the jolt back to reality. No surprises here, but this is the phase where most ideas sit abandoned, left by the roadside.
This is the phase I employ you to be vigilant and ground your dreams into action. Take baby steps here. Be resilient when facing the challenges that may present themselves when you start taking action. These ideas that have successfully passed through the sweeper in the Head phase and have earned their right to be in the Hand stage. So, slip into gear and step on the accelerator! In this activity, prioritise the ideas that have passed through unscathed.

_____
_____
_____

You now have the beginnings of some specific goals. Record them in your journal, on your vision board or at your desk, anywhere really, where they can be seen; so you can envision your goals through your Kombi's windscreen on the journey ahead.

I love the Heart-Head-Hand model, as it bridges a lovely gap between imagination and reality. It provides hope for the dreamers knowing that their ideas are heard, satisfaction for the realists that they get to sort and cull and excitement for the critic who can magnify the options and ask the tough questions.

Your windscreen of vision will be that much wider and clearer when you travel your journey with great faith in yourself and your vision. You know yourself best and, if you choose to, you are free to crank up the volume of that inner voice; your inner guide and co-pilot.

Choose a system or collection of systems which work best for you. Remember you have a toolbox of systems to choose from:

- SMART Goals - SMART is an acronym that stands for Specific, Measurable, Achievable, Realistic, and Timely. SMART goals are used to assist in goal setting. They help to focus your efforts and increase successful goal achievement.

- To do lists - The old-fashioned handwritten pen and paper lists, displayed in a predominant place as a reminder of your goals.

- Diaries - Electronic or paper diaries provide a visual reminder of time frames for the achievement of specific goals.

- Heart - Head - Hand model - As outlined above.

- Vision boards - A vision board is a visual representation of your goals and dreams, using a collage of words, quotes and images.

- Accountability buddies - An accountability partner is part coach, part cheerleader. They are someone you choose to help guide and motivate you; help you move closer to achieving your goals and dreams.

- Gearbox system - Use the gearbox system from this chapter to step out the individual gear changes you'll need to make to pick up speed and gain momentum towards your dreams.

Once you've chosen from your toolbox, you are one step closer to embarking on the trip of a lifetime. Whether your destination is known or in the hands of the universe, be bold, be brave and most importantly hold the vision and trust in what lies beyond your windscreen.

Trip notes

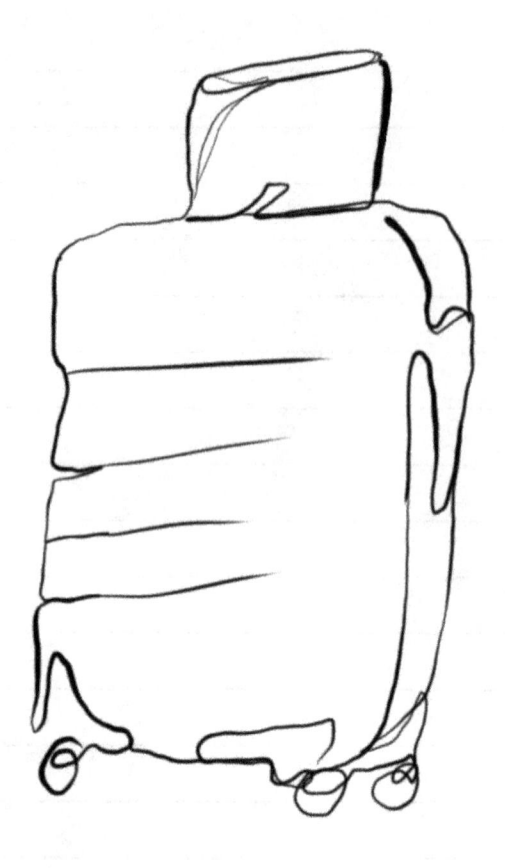

*Focus on what you can control,
And don't waste energy
on the things that you cannot.*

UNKNOWN

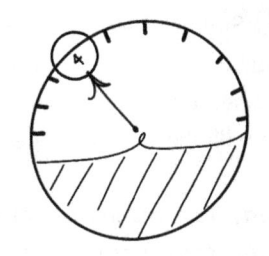

The Baggage

The Baggage

Years ago, I enjoyed the most insightful conversation with a middle-aged Buddhist nun. My friend and I were attending a weekend meditation retreat in the Blue Mountains, west of Sydney. We had enjoyed a morning of outdoor Tai Chi, a session of silent walking meditation and a delicious vegetarian lunch. Before we headed into the afternoon session, we were encouraged to indulge in some friendly conversations with the quietly gathered nuns.

Michelle and I made our way towards the pot of freshly brewed tea, where we met the gaze of an older nun, perhaps in her mid-sixties. A sense of awkwardness overtook me, as I felt all my suppressed words from the silent morning sessions rapidly drain from my body.
What could I possibly say to a Buddhist nun? I tried to shake my nerves and was thankful when I heard Michelle lead the conversation, allowing me time to steady myself and regain composure. The nun asked Michelle if she was married. I took a deep breath and hoped that my long inhalation would somehow make me invisible. This was a conversation I knew would be difficult for my friend, and one that I thought she would prefer to have privately.

As other small groups buzzed happily around me, I became boxed in with no escape. So, I took a gulp of my lukewarm tea and listened as Michelle began her story, meticulously crafting her words to form an accurate summary of her current marital situation.

Her husband was dying; a cruel drawn out death under cancer's watchful eye. The nun listened with a patient ear and an open heart to Michelle's story.
I scanned her face for any hint of emotion. She showed none of the traditional emotions that I expected, having just listened to a heartbreaking story.
There was an absence of tears, no bitten lip and no distracted looks. Instead, she held the space beautifully and did not falter in her demeanor. I could only stand in wonder.

When my friend finished, the nun took a long considered breath, not unlike my own, and simply said "Cut it and let it go!" We looked at each other, dumbfounded! We couldn't believe what had befallen our ears. Our senses were numbed by her immunity to drama.

And just like that, my dearest friend had been granted permission to move on, to crudely slice her story and forge a different ending. The nun must have sensed our doubt and disbelief, as she went on to explain that Michelle's husband's suffering was not hers to bear alone. The suffering she was experiencing, although sad, was hers to control. The choices she was making and those she was avoiding, were completely her responsibility.

Michelle and I never spoke of it again. I savoured those words and adopted them as if they were mine, into a daily mantra. For these wise, yet simple words fit like a glove and danced magically in my thoughts. They were the scissors to the strings which bound my gathered insecurities, seeking permission to be cut loose and fly away: 'Cut it and let it go!'

What Is Excess Baggage?

Life can be challenging, there's no debating that! As social beings, we live in a world where people, situations and our environment challenges us, on a daily basis. Nothing matters more than our strength of character and how we choose to respond to life's emotional baggage, which I like to refer to as excess baggage. This is the unwanted baggage weighing your Kombi down along your life journey.

Excess baggage includes the insecurities and hang-ups that intensify and accelerate over the span of our lives. It is a collective term for past experiences which are begging for attention and resolution. Our excess baggage can influence and undermine our growth and our happiness, and halt us on our journey.

Collecting and accumulating excess baggage is normal and can be one of our most helpful teachers. Dealing with excess baggage can be as complicated or as simple as you choose.

A heads-up though, it may require the intensity of a *head on* intervention, if you're truly ready to release yourself from its clutches.

Each morning we are faced with a new beginning, a set of new choices and decisions to make to get us through to tomorrow. While we may not be responsible for all the baggage we carry, we have an obligation and duty to ourselves to respond to how we carry the burdens we stow in our excess baggage.

As we navigate this world, we absorb our experiences and choose where to 'store' them. After all, if we are truly present in our lives, then it's only natural that we throw some items into our handbags, backpacks, suitcases, or into excess baggage. The baggage worth keeping will sit comfortably within the space you allocate it. It's only when the baggage becomes overloaded and too heavy to carry, too painful to look at, that we must accept the invitation to repack our bags. This often means reassessing our behaviours and making necessary adjustments and changes to our actions. This can be quite simple but never easy!

The True Cost Of Our Excess Baggage

For many years, two of my closest friends and I would make the annual pilgrimage to Broadbeach, Queensland for a girls' getaway. We always went during the summer, which meant packing lightly for our endless sun filled days and planned shopping trips. However, each year as we checked our baggage in, we would watch the flight attendant place a bold yellow sticker on my suitcase which read: HEAVY. Thank goodness I never incurred a fee for the additional baggage I was carrying, but the risk was always present, looming in the rear view mirror.

Our excess baggage can cost us terribly in life; physically, emotionally and financially. The cost will be different for each person. In my workshops, women have shared the price that they have paid for holding on to excess baggage instead of reassessing and releasing.

These include;
- missed opportunities
- half hearted attempts at living
- held grudges
- harboured anger
- financial hardships
- lingering jealousy

The energy spent pondering, analysing and even justifying the presence of our excess baggage inevitably eats into our precious time, something we don't have in ample supply.
I love the phrase, *Holding onto anger is like drinking poison and expecting the other person to die.* Anger is the ultimate hijacker; an exhausting process with zero gain, only pain! Anger is not the only thief looking for tired, vulnerable travelers. My literal excess check in baggage equates to my obsession with control, or more specifically, my need to have a reservoir of options, which has its costly price.

Whenever I pack for a holiday, whether it be for a week, a month or longer,
I knowingly pack with options as my priority. When packing for our annual getaway to Broadbeach, there would always be an abundance of considerations.
If it was cold, I would need jackets (note the plural). If I was struggling with the heat, I would need singlets, one for each day plus one. If we were walking, I would need joggers but also some flats. Then there were the going out shoes, the ones for dinner, the ones for dancing. Despite knowing that our accommodation provided both a hairdryer and straightener, I still packed both. There was an abundance of ifs which no doubt weighted my suitcase heavily.

I can't help but wonder, how different my holiday experiences would have been without the extra clothes and the extra weighty options!

If I had stopped micro-managing my life, my experiences and even my baggage, I could have loosened up a little and enjoyed a more relaxed journey.

How Does Excess Baggage Show Up In Life?

Excess baggage may show up in our life as a sad and sorry mess or a neat and tidy niggle. Regardless, it has an uncanny way of making its presence felt as it reverberates around us and echoes within our heads. Baggage can manifest as controlling, micro-managing, perfectionism, regrets, unresolved differences, people pleasing and constant comparisons.

So, why do we hang onto our excess baggage like we're holding onto dear life? By clinging on to our baggage, we are allowing the monotonous reruns of our dramas, insecurities and hangups. Our baggage can forge deep roots into our past, making it difficult or next to impossible to live in the present.

Only when we commit to letting go of the binds that hold us back, can we truly be free to focus on the here and now and prepare for the journey which awaits us.

Ignition Exercise
Lightening the Load Of Excess Baggage

Step One
Make an itemised list - as long as you wish - of the excess baggage you are currently carrying. Include the small items, as well as the uncomfortable and the weighty ones. Don't hold back because even the act of writing them down is one step closer towards the 'Cut it and let it go' release experience.

_____   _____
_____   _____
_____   _____
_____   _____
_____   _____

Step Two
Identify the baggage that no longer nourishes and empowers you. You may like to highlight, circle or cross out the items on your list. Have a strong resolve here to commit to the culling process. Imagine being gifted with a helium balloon and a marker. Which items would be graffitied over your balloon and then forced to await their much needed release?

Step Three
After writing all your excess baggage concerns across your balloon, visualise the release of that unwanted mass of latex.
Imagine the liberation, the weightlessness, the freedom!
As you are visualising the release ask yourself,
how does this feel?

_____

_____

Over time, I have devised 3 simple questions that I pose to myself during self pity parties that I occasionally hold.

When stubbornly head butting an insecurity or hang up. I encourage you to ask yourself these same questions;
    1. Does this nourish me?
    2. Does this empower me?
    3. When I let this go, how will I feel?

> **Does this nourish me?**
> **Does this empower me?**
> **When I let this go,**
> **how will I feel?**

Some of us lavish more attention on our fears than on spontaneous impulses.
The fear of failure can be debilitating,
yet sometimes it's easier to sit in the comfort of discomfort.
That is until you decide to question the baggage and challenge it with vigour and gusto.
If you ask a big enough why, you will receive big enough responses.

Internal Dialogue – Heart vs Ego

We all have an inner voice, the silent words which formulate our thoughts, memories, plans and responses.
Although researchers estimate that we spend at least half of our lives talking to ourselves, this varies from person to person. Here is an example of some internal dialogue that may take place if I was to question a chosen piece of my baggage that I was ready to release.

EGO: Clare-Ann, I notice that you are holding onto the hurt you experienced from the ending of a friendship which dissolved almost 10 years ago.
What do you call that baggage?

HEART: I call it guilt. I could or should have committed more attention to that friendship.

EGO: Does the guilt nourish you?

HEART: No it doesn't!

EGO: Does the guilt empower you?

HEART: Definitely not!

EGO: When you let go of the guilt, how will you feel?

HEART: I will feel lighter and finally be able to accept that the friendship dissolved for several reasons, most of them beyond my control.

Ignition Exercise
Release Insecurity

Now it's your turn to try your hand at recording your own internal dialogue. Think of a niggling voice of insecurity that you would like to free from the baggage carrier, which sits above your Kombi. Remember you need to pack lightly for this journey and need to declutter and 'lighten the load' before you head off. You may use the Heart vs Ego dialogue, as I did, and imagine that the Ego is the interviewer and your Heart is the responder, your true self. Don't get too bogged down in the details, just choose an easy framework to set out your internal dialogue.

For example:

EGO : I've noticed that you have been holding on to _____ and I'd like you to tell me a little more about that.

HEART: Yes, I'm aware of that and I think it's called _____ because I have difficulty in _____

_____

_____

_____

Now it's your turn!

Ego _____
_____

Heart _____
_____

Ego _____
_____

Heart _____
_____

Ego _____
_____

Heart _____
_____

<u>Key Reasons We Hold On To Excess Baggage</u>

There are some key factors which may be holding you back from releasing your excess baggage: fear; ignorance; guilt; regret; and your story.

<u>Fear:</u>
Fear is a primal emotional response to triggers such as the threat of harm, whether it be physical, emotional, real or imagined. I won't go into too much detail here, as I have dedicated a whole chapter to fear later in the book. Needless to say, fear can become the enemy when trauma and/or grief have not been addressed with the sensitivity and time needed. Baggage tarnished with fear may find you avoiding not only day-to-day tasks but, sadly, life!

Ignorance:
Like so many of us mere mortals, you may be oblivious or ignorant to the enormity of baggage piling upon your shoulders, bearing down and slowly wearing you flat. A psychologist friend of mine who deals specifically with clients diagnosed with PTSD shared her insight with me on the depths of emotional baggage and the destructive nature on the sufferer as well as their families. She explained that a sufferer of PTSD may harbour their grief and their trauma in the darkest of ports within their minds. There it lays dormant, festering quietly like an abscess, politely waiting to erupt.

The sufferer continues on the daily treadmill of life, maybe experiencing bouts of stress or slight anxiousness, but nothing too dramatic. And then one day it hits and boy does it hit. Like a high-speed bowling ball hurtling down the alley, sending pins in all directions.

The suitcase of excess baggage stored so carefully in the wardrobe of secrets, for however long, is thrown open revealing all.

Regrets and Guilt:
Regrets and guilt are forms of punishment which hold you prisoner to past mistakes of the head and heart. Accept that imperfections and poor judgements happen and are often made by good people with admirable intentions. Make peace with those you have hurt, particularly yourself, and vow to move on with greater wisdom and insight.

The Stories We Tell Ourselves:
We all have a story and as storytellers, we can fall into the complacent trap of exhausting re-runs of our dramas. If the story you're running is growing tired and predictably cliche, close it, dump it and choose a fresh start, a new book with a strong spine! You are the author of your life; choose carefully how you write your story.

Preparing To Let Go

While I have devoted numerous hours to researching the *why* of letting go, I would like to share some personal and practical tips on *how* to kick start the process - some gear change systems. I liken this process to spring cleaning a room, a favourite room in your home. I invite you to participate in a spring clean in the upcoming Ignition Exercise. This will act as a simple catalyst for the final step in this chapter - preparing to get out of your own way!

When the spring cleaning bug hits me, it flies in a swarm and irritates me to the point of action. I've heard the old wives' tale, that spring cleaning suggests a woman may be clucky, or pregnant. For me it's neither; it's more of an opportunity for a deep cleanse of my mind.

In the summer of 2019, Australia was hit with extreme heat conditions, which resulted in catastrophic bushfires around our country. Left with little to do but keep cool inside, I binge watched Marie Kondo's Netflix episodes, in which she enlightened her viewers with her best decluttering tips. I quickly became hooked, drawn in by the simplicity of her methods and the incredible results she achieved. I became an instant minimalist devotee and set about decluttering every room in our home. This gung-ho approach worried my family as they observed from the sidelines, wondering how long I could sustain my efforts.
I felt like I was performing back-to-back live shows, seven days a week! It was exhausting and overwhelming, yet somehow completely rewarding. While I don't suggest that you take on such the mammoth task of decluttering every aspect of your baggage in one day, I do recommend focusing on one compartment at a time, one simple step at a time!

So, with the inspiring words of decluttering expert and award winning author, Marie Kondo, I encourage you to consider her phrase 'Does this spark joy?' as you shift gears through your mountain of physical and emotional baggage.

The following Ignition Exercise is an opportunity to use the momentum of cleaning out your physical belongings to help shift emotional baggage you no longer want to store on the roof of your Kombi.

Ignition Exercise

SPRING CLEANING YOUR MIND AND YOUR HOME

YOUR MIND	YOUR HOME
Focus on one area of your life, preferably an area containing significant baggage (love, friendship, work, family). The area in my life that I'm going to focus on is	Pick a room. The room I'm going to focus on is ....
Record all the emotions (nourishing or disempowering) that come to mind when you ask yourself: When I think of this area of my life I feel; * * *	Unpack the room, emptying the contents into a central place.
Record your thoughts (nourishing or disempowering) as you address each emotion when you ask yourself: I feel .... because .... I feel .... because.. I feel .... because..	Look at the mound of 'stuff' in front of you. How does it make you feel? I feel .... when I look at all the 'stuff' in front of me.
Write a list of the nourishing vs the disempowering thoughts and emotions associated with your baggage Remember the 3 important questions at this stage are: 1. Does this nourish me? 2. Does this empower me? 3. When I let this go, how will I feel?	Start the epic sorting into piles: ; **FOR KEEPS & LET IT GO** When holding each item ask yourself, Does this item have a story? Does the story nourish me?
Consider the thoughts and emotions that you have identified as disempowering. Are you ready to send them off with a Cut it & let it go farewell? If yes, imagine writing these thoughts on a helium balloon and sending them off into the universe and eventually the Black Hole, where they belong!	Bundle the Let it Go pile into a garbage bag to be rehomed, regifted or recycled.
Consider the thoughts and emotions that you identified as nurturing (remember not all baggage is disempowering). It can be there to serve as a reminder of a lesson, an experience or both. Decide on how you want to carry them. Will they be packed neatly into the back of your mind or do they sit towards the frontal cortex, guiding from a comfortable distance?	Repack the items you want to keep into their rightful place. They have survived your ruthless cull. They can now rest easy for another 12 months or so.
Acknowledge yourself and the commitment you have shown in the decluttering of your suitcase of weighted baggage. Congratulations! Now it's time to reward yourself - free of judgement, free of guilt!	Step back in your decluttered room and marvel at the commitment it has taken to reach that point. Congratulations! Now it's time to reward yourself!

Getting Out Of Your Way

Letting go of emotional baggage takes time but it also takes understanding, acceptance and forgiveness. Along the way we learn to accept the things we can and can't control, in turn providing us with the first few steps towards moving on.

Steven Covey, the well known author of *The 7 Habits of Highly Effective People*, devised *The Circle of Concern vs The Circle of Influence* model. It provides a visual representation of the things that concern us, that we have no control over, versus the influence we can have over the things that we can control. Furthermore, it shines a light on where we are choosing to focus our energy, either on our concerns or our influences.

Imagine the difference in your life if you pumped all your time and energy into that which you *could* control? Imagine being able to unpack the suitcase holding your baggage, the one bulging at the seams, with the damaged zipper from overuse?

Imagine having the task of sifting through your unpacked baggage; ruthlessly discarding the items that no longer support, guide or transform you? Imagine then repacking your compact and manageable hand luggage, which held only a selection of items you have the power to influence! Liberating, huh?

What lies ahead is a journey filled with endless possibilities and growth.
There is an open road begging to be explored. Whether you set off on your own or with your tribe, go forth with a minimalist's mindset. For what you need along the way, you will find. The universe has a way of blessing us when we need her the most. And when she is unable to provide, improvisation may become your new fuel.

Getting out of your own way is a fun phrase which invites you to take yourself less seriously. It involves the quietening of the ego and the filtering of the doubts. This phrase sounds simple yet is sometimes difficult to do. Getting out of your own way could potentially be the permission note you seek to jump start your journey, pass through the toll gates, and get on your way.

Marcus Aurelius, one of the last Good Emperors of Rome reigned from 161–180CE. In one of his well known and loved writings, Aurelius suggested
'What stands in the way becomes the way.'
The path before us is messy and laden with speed bumps, a highway of challenges and of course, our baggage.
Depending on our attitudes and character, we may seek detours, diversions and even short cuts. Marcus Aurelius denotes that perhaps the winding road holds our growth and greatest achievements.

When you get out of your way, you are in essence allowing the journey to continue on its natural flow, and your personal growth to gain traction and momentum. Then, as you face each obstacle, you can trust you are equipped with the wisdom and experience gained from hand selected lessons learned over time. Coupled with a deep sense of self and strength of character, you curiously forge on, excitedly anticipating the feeling of empowerment on the open road!

Minimise Baggage, Maximise Adventure

I can highly recommend checklists (it must be the teacher in me) to ensure that you stick to your plan of keeping it simple. As experience and a little dose of embarrassment have taught me, simplicity and a sense of adventure are the
keys to packing a manageable bag. When you minimise your distractions and baggage, you maximise the chance of adventure and spark along your journey.

Here is a toolbox of simple ideas to help get out of your own way and keep things simple:

- Choose carefully the five people you surround yourself with, because you become the average of them (more on this in Chapter 8).

- Think about the language you use and remember that you are the author of your life story. Are you operating from a tank half full or tank half empty mentality? Shifting from *If I could* to *When I do!* can be very powerful.

- Hold some intense Q & A sessions with yourself. Ask big *whys* to gain big responses. Are you holding onto excuses like you are holding onto your excess baggage?

- Try a new approach. Go to bed earlier, get up earlier, exercise before work, replace sweets with fruit. What new action could you incorporate to shake up an old pattern?

- Break the TV fuzz. If you are tired of hearing your sad story on repeat, then chances are, so are others. It's time to change the channel!

- Check in and see if you are focusing predominantly on the influences that you can control rather than the concerns beyond your power.

Excess baggage is a collection of our experiences and responses to events from our past. They influence our thoughts, our behaviour and our actions, based on the importance we place on them.

As human beings, or human becomings, we are seekers of knowledge and students of life. We are always on a journey towards becoming who we need and desire to be. We have a commitment to ourselves to travel this journey with emotions that fuel us with courage and hope. Life is short, so let the journey be fun.

Let go of the emotions that no longer nourish and empower you and give them a send off that they deserve. Accept and understand that the journey ahead is littered with speed bumps and potholes. Thankfully there will be beautiful views to admire as you are travelling through life. Be kind to yourself and adjust your seat if you need to. Catch one last glimpse in the rear-view mirror of what was and then focus ahead on your windscreen, on what is to become of your journey.

Trip notes

Courage is knowing what not to fear.

PLATO

The Brakes

The Brakes

Aviophobia is an abnormal and irrational fear of flying. It is an anxiety disorder which can cause heightened awareness, sweaty palms, nausea and shortness of breath. And while statistics suggest that on average, people report their first fear of flying 'attack' at the age of 27, I believe I acquired my phobia at the age of eighteen, in 1989, after enduring a horrendously turbulent hour and a half flight.

Travelling as a group of three, my coach, my acrobatic partner and I were making our way to the Sports Acrobatics World Titles in Riga, Russia. We were representing Australia in a sport which was relatively new to our country, yet fairly well established amongst the Eastern European countries.

After two weeks of combined training and sightseeing in London, we had arrived in Moscow, eagerly awaiting our connecting flight to Riga, the capital of Latvia. We excitedly boarded a well known and established Russian airline in the early afternoon on a crisp September day. We made our way to our seats, carefully edging past other passengers who were busy stowing their cabin luggage.

The seats were a tired, cheap royal blue like a worn leather lounge. I remember sinking into my seat, wondering if perhaps it was broken and in need of a more supportive frame. I yanked on the seatbelt which seemed to have withdrawn itself into the saggy crease where the backrest met the base.

Not wanting to dive too eagerly into the back of the seat, for fear of what I may find, I eventually managed to release the belt and secure it around my lap.

The takeoff and first few minutes of the flight were uneventful and I relaxed into my space, donned my headphones and listened to my Sony CD Walkman. The soothing tunes of Richard Marks gently softened my mood and reminded me of my boyfriend waiting for me back home.

A short time into the flight, we began being thrown around like rag dolls in an overzealous industrial washing machine. Limp with fear, I felt the colour very quickly drain from my face. I was terrified; a sitting duck in a nightmarish sideshow alley, I felt like I was the target as the turbulence took its aim.

We had a Russian translator, Annika, who was assigned to our team. She was young and diminutive, with the features of a perfectly crafted Babooshka doll. Her long blonde hair was swept into a conservative ponytail, which I had noticed earlier, swung with an easy rhythm. She spoke with eloquence and finesse, beautifully blending her native tongue with an impressive mastery of English.

As the turbulence gathered momentum, Annika nervously peeped her head between the two seats in front of me. I could sense the unease in her face as she struggled to compose herself. She looked me straight in the eyes and said in her thick Russian accent, "Start praying!" I was only 18, but I distinctly remember designing the front page of the Australian Newspaper, including headlines and images. I grieved for my parents, having to read of my last moments.

The lights of the cabin continued to flicker on and off with a loose rhythm that not only fueled my angst but lulled me into a premeditative state. Obviously, we survived the flight, but still to this day, I have never felt so afraid of my own mortality and felt so morbidly alone.

We stayed in Riga for over a week and managed a few sightseeing experiences in between our scheduled training and competition sessions. I remember looking towards the sky and wondering if I would ever experience a Russian blue sky or if they were a rare phenomenon. Each day, I would playfully beg our acrobatics' coach to allow me to return to Moscow by train when the time came. But behind my jovial requests was a festering knot of tangled angst slowly driving me crazy.

As all true aviophobia experts suggest, one must confront their fears head on and do exactly what their mind *doesn't* want them to do.

So, in my case, as fortune had it, I was not only made to board the flight back to Moscow, but I then had a subsequent flight home to Australia to prepare for. There was no avoiding the fact we had to cross the Indian Ocean.

It was some years later - upon hearing the incredibly wise words of Madame Marie Currie - *Nothing in life is to be feared, it is only to be understood* - that I sought the information and tools to help understand and cure my phobia. After all, knowledge is power.

Armed with powerful fresh knowledge, I developed the belief that I could take control of the issues that I had around flying.
I wanted to nip my fear in the bud to prevent it from blossoming into a phobia which could potentially limit or prevent any further overseas travel.

My research led me to several successfully proven psychological based courses, utilising multi-layered theories, mechanical engineered explanations and simulated practices. They all tempted me and I was curious enough to ask a fellow aviophobic friend of mine to enrol in a Sydney course. As fortune had it, each time I went to register my interest, I would balk at the exorbitant course fees, forcing me to try a different tack.

I took the tough approach, deciding that the financial investment would be far better spent on booking an actual flight. Fear and I had a date - more an intervention - that would see us confronting our issues 33,000 feet above sea level. There would only be one winner, and that would be me! I will reveal my action plan later in this chapter.

When fear jumps up out of nowhere like a threatening obstacle on the road, our natural response is to apply the brakes. Fear might show up in our lives like an unwanted rattle in our Kombi; obnoxiously irritating and begging to be silenced. Eventually, the rattle turns into a persistent clang requiring investigation, and this means applying the brakes to investigate! Although somewhat annoying, the clanging is there to alert us to a problem or emotion that needs our attention.

Whilst brakes are an essential feature in your Kombi, they won't propel you forward if you ride them the whole way.

When we first learn to drive, we are usually instructed to hover over the brakes when approaching intersections, roundabouts and other interruptions in our path. Shadowing the brakes in this way means that we're cautious and in control.
This is an ideal approach and ensures assertive driving behaviour.

Excessive use of your brakes, however, will wear them down and they'll need regular replacing along the way! Along your journey, you will no doubt test your brakes and you will be tested by them.

What Is Fear?

The word fear comes from the Greek word - *phóbos,* meaning 'fear' or 'morbid fear'. It is a negative sensation prompted by a perceived threat. It occurs in response to a specific stimulus, such as pain or the threat of danger.

Fear brings the innate ability to recognise danger and flee from it, freeze with it or confront it - also known as the flight, fight or freeze response. Although we no longer experience the same threats of danger, harm or extinction as our ancestors, our primitive desire for flight, fight or freeze remains within us.

Fear is an inevitable part of who we are as human beings. We are hard wired to experience fear. This neurological fear system in our brains which once helped us to survive, now often limits and controls our lives.

We fear events that are inevitable (ageing, death and being alone), we fear actions that we need to take (making decisions, getting fit, changing jobs, asserting ourselves, speaking in public), and we fear experiencing emotions (rejection, vulnerability, exclusion, failure).

Within those levels are sub levels, making fear seem messy and too challenging to deal with. Understandably, we develop avoidance techniques, such as procrastination. As mentioned in the chapter on goals, procrastination is always prepped and ready for action. Procrastination is fear's lifeline, a devoted detour around an awkward array of obstacles and excuses.

Procrastination is like driving around with your handbrake up. It's not only pointless but harmful to the mechanisms underneath the Kombi's bonnet. It's an avoidance tactic with the sole purpose of prolonging the inevitable.
Don't be fooled by procrastination's promises.

> **Procrastination is fear's lifeline, a devoted detour around an awkward array of obstacles and excuses.**

What appears at first to be cautionary, may end up becoming a broader problem, prolonging your journey and possibly resulting in your Kombi being deemed unroadworthy and thus undrivable for a while.

Fear vs Phobias

Fear is an instinctive and emotional response to a real or perceived threat. It plays an important role in our lives. It is there to keep us safe when facing possible danger and harmful situations. Under normal circumstances and armed with coping strategies, fear can be managed using logic and reason.
At the time of writing *A Woman's Way*, we are all facing uncertain times.
We are in the midst of COVID-19, a worldwide pandemic with levelled restrictions and gradual lockdowns in place. With universal uncertainty, it's hardly surprising that people have become fearful. The panic buying of toilet paper and pantry items, as well as the constant media hype bombarding us, is relentless.

For many people the fear surrounding this pandemic has become catastrophic, and some people may have experienced spiraling into overwhelm and panic. Logic and reason need to prevail. By staying informed from reliable sources, following recommended hygiene guidelines and focusing on what we *can* control, we will feel more empowered. With knowledge comes power, and hence the ability to be proactive and starve the fear.

A phobia twists a fear response into something often difficult or seemingly impossible to control. Phobias are anxiety disorders where the associated fear becomes excessive and grossly out of proportion to the object, event or situation. Unlike fear, the anxiety someone may experience with a phobia can be so strong that it interferes with their quality of life. For example, Agoraphobics have a fear of being in open, crowded spaces, which may result in them having a fear of leaving the house.

What Do We Fear?

After reading numerous online articles and studies completed around the world, the same top ten fears kept recurring in my research.
There are many things that people fear but here is a snapshot of the most common and universal fears, in no particular order.

- Public Speaking
- Germs
- Confined or open spaces
- Thunder & lightning
- Animals, including snakes, spiders and dogs
- Heights
- Needles
- Flying
- Failure
- Death

As I've shared with you at the beginning of this chapter, I have a fear of flying where I become nervous and jittery when I board a flight. I try to manage my symptoms with meditative practices, a preflight meal and listening to calming downloaded playlists. However, during episodes of mild to severe turbulence, my fear becomes a phobia; I lose the ability to control my emotions and I sometimes start to shake, rock, sweat and cry.
Whilst my phobia has yet to reach a level where I will avoid travel altogether, it did reach a point where I needed to seek expert advice.

Ignition Exercise
Exploring Fear and Phobia

Do you have a fear that triggers an emotional response/s?
What is it? What is your navigation system to overcome your fear?

_____
_____

Do you have any phobias?
(Remember a phobia is the next level of fear, where the anxiety associated is so strong that it has impacted upon your life).
What is it? What does it prevent you from doing in your life?

_____
_____
_____
_____

<u>Types Of Fears</u>

Fears may be classified into two main categories: external and internal fears. External fears or phobias are triggered by an outside source, such as spiders, ghosts, heights and water.
Since the source of fear is easier to identify than an internal fear, one can remain hopeful of finding an alternative way to confront the trigger or fear.

Similar to external fears, an internal fear has triggers which come from an outside source which produce internal fears and reactions. Self doubt, questioning one's ability to do something or a fear of failure are all examples of internal fears. Internal fears fester from internal thoughts, rather than facing the fear front on. They are led and fueled by emotions such as rejection, vulnerability and inadequacy.

This type of fear often impacts one's ability to interact within their work or social environment because they live in fear of judgement. Fear of failure may show up in your life as a reluctance to nominate yourself for a promotion, or a new initiative in the workplace. Self doubt and vulnerability may become heavy burdens which prevent attendance at social gatherings, forming new connections with others and even committing to long term relationships.

Fear vs Worry

Worrying is like praying for something you don't want to happen.
ANON

Fear is generally an involuntary emotion, whereas *worry* is a choice.
Fear can be a useful emotion which keeps you away from danger.
Worry is a useless head-mind state that keeps you trapped in *what if* thinking.
It almost always arises when you are not getting what you want. Your brain is receiving fear messages that you are unaware of. Like a bored child, an overactive mind will shift into the gear of make believe and drive through the potholes of what-ifs.

As a teacher, I've spent a fair chunk of time listening to children's worries.
In my second year of university, I remember making a pact with a lecturer to never say to a child who was worried, "Don't worry!" We all laughed while giving the verbal promise but to this day, I can honestly say that those words have never passed my lips. Children worry, as do adults, and while it's important to address our worries and deal with them, simply telling someone not to worry may help you more than it helps them.

A simple strategy I like to use with children, and you may find useful as well, is what I have named *Let's Walk it Through*. Although somewhat basic in structure, I have found it highly effective when children (and even adults) are stuck in an 'overthinking' spiral. It's a somewhat comical way of confronting stubborn worries by talking through hypotheticals.

Here's an example of the Let's Walk it Through strategy:

Child: I'm worried about putting my hand up in class.
Me: I'm curious. Why?
Child: Because kids will laugh at me.
Me: And if they laugh at you, what will happen?
Child: I will get embarrassed.
Me: And once you're embarrassed what will happen?
Child: I will turn red and probably cry.
Me: And once you have turned red and had a cry what will happen?
Child: (At this point, the child will usually pause because they've never been encouraged to think past their uncomfortable emotions. But I usually forge on, but gently).
Me: So, you are now embarrassed and had a cry, what will happen next?
Child: The teacher will probably help me or tell me to get a tissue or have a drink.
Me: And once you have had a drink and wiped your eyes, what will happen?
Child: My friends will check if I'm ok.
Me: And will you be ok?
Child: Yes.
Me: Will you be okay to try again and put your hand up?
Child: At this point the child normally allows a smile to sneak across their face, an acknowledgement that whilst their worry paid a short visit, they were able to take control of it and not let it take control of them.

Feel free to try the *Let's Walk it Through* technique. Remember to keep your responses simple and honest to keep you on course.

In 1988, Bobby McFerrin released a popular song titled *Don't Worry Be Happy* with simple yet catchy lyrics. Through his lyrical poetry, McFerrin encourages us to accept that life is full of troubles but by focusing on them, they will only double. In essence, his lyrics suggest that what we focus on grows.

As a gardener, I understand this concept perfectly, so applying it to everyday life should be just as simple. Ask any gardener what makes a garden grow and they will most likely answer water. Obviously love, time, effort and money are also contributing factors, but having been through heavy water restrictions brought on from a few years of drought, water truly is the key.

During these thirsty times, my garden had to rely on the random offerings from our shower buckets and directed trickles from watering cans. The flowers I tended to the most, flourished while others could no longer sustain my reduced attention and simply died. Similarly, the fears we focus on and feed will flourish, unless we make a conscious decision to recognise them and then bid them farewell by excluding them from our thoughts and attention.

Facing Fear

By facing your fears, putting your foot on the brake and navigating the fear obstacles in front of you, you are creating an opportunity to be open to greater freedom. The freedom to live your life on your terms, the way you want to experience it! You are allowing yourself to unfold into your true potential, to experience who you really are!

As you journey along, you will notice that old patterns, beliefs and behaviour will fade into the rear view mirror, as you begin to experience the truth of the effortless freedom ride that you have available.

The exciting news is that we do have a certain amount of control over how we choose to confront and deal with our fears. Firstly, you need to learn to differentiate between whether your fears are rational or irrational.
Similarly, when you're driving along and the dashboard illuminates, you need to be curious enough to question whether the light warrants a need to proceed with caution, to stop or to abandon your plans altogether.

Smoke coming from beneath your bonnet elicits a rational fear, an instant trigger to stop and seek assistance. However, the faulty brake light that keeps flashing on your dashboard, may simply reveal a faulty light, not faulty brakes.

Using Fear As An Engine

Well known author, Paulo Coelho encourages us to use fear as an engine rather than as a brake. When I reflect on these wise words, I think of the adrenalin that fear often produces, and how that can be harnessed to make me dig deeper and rise even stronger. Elite athletes have mastered the art of feeling the fear and pushing through.
Daredevils thrive on the thrill; first seeking the risk, accepting the danger and then enjoying the buzz. That's not to say that we must all put the pedal to the metal and break speed records in our Kombis. I'm simply suggesting these examples are 'fuel for thought' for us more cautious Kombi drivers.

The last flight I took was in 2018. I decided that enough was enough.
I needed to take charge and show my mind who was boss. After all, what we resist persists and what we befriend transcends. The powerful acronym for FEAR, Face Everything and Rise, is how I decided to confront my fear of flying.
I needed to adopt a step-by-step system, so I could work my way through the gearbox to alleviate the angst around the physical and emotional idea of flying.

My hope is that the steps I have outlined below may be adapted and personalised to suit your fear or phobia needs. Whether it be visiting the dentist, speaking in front of an audience or boarding a roller coaster, your process may require several gear changes, and a commitment to rising up over that mountain of fear.

Here is an example that walks you through my system that I used to tackle my fear of flying. Once you have read thorough the steps, allow some time to write down your own gear box steps. If at any point you feel overwhelmed or triggered, stop, breathe, get up if necessary and seek support from a friend or medical expert if needed.

❝ What we resist persists and what we befriend transcends. ❞

Facing Fear Head On

Name the Fear: _____Fear of Flying_____

STEP 1 Create An Anchor
I anchor* a positive mantra about the one thing that I'm looking forward to once I reach my destination. For example, *I can't wait to order room service,* or *I can't wait to hear the waves at night,* or *I can't wait to hug my dog* or *I can't wait to walk barefoot in my garden.*

I then feel deeply into that excitement, amplifying all the sensory delights attached to that strong visual representation.

• *An anchor is a positive tool in the form of a thought, image or phrase that grounds you, within your body and mind. It is something you can hold on to metaphorically when you feel overwhelmed and in need of calming yourself. Similar to a ship's anchor, it is there to hold you in place and to provide you with strength in times of need.*

STEP 2 Test The Anchor
As I approach the plane, stow my luggage, buckle into my seat and listen to the safety demonstration, I test my anchor by reciting my mantra and I repeat it until I can feel it fully.

STEP 3 Be Aware Of Mind Jacking
I ensure that I'm aware of my mind's desire to mind jack my calmness. As my mind tries to look for signs of impending danger coming from the pilot's words, the beeping sounds in the cabin, the number of empty seats or the chatter of the attendants, I call bullshit and shut it down. If necessary, I repeat my mantra and its powerful visualisation.

STEP 4 One Step Closer
As the cabin door closes, as the gate moves away and the plane starts taxiing, I remind myself that I am one step closer to experiencing my anchored mantra. For example: *I am one step closer to walking barefoot in my garden.*

STEP 5 Embrace The Fear & The Adrenalin Rush
I have a specific playlist for my take off routine (odd I know, but it helps).

The Chainsmokers song *Something Like This* is my song of choice. I prepare the song to coincide with the adrenalin rush I experience with the sudden thrust from idle standing to the accelerated charge down the runway. It's difficult to explain the exhilaration but it's like I'm taunting my comfort zone, throwing wild rebellion to the wind and saying "Later!"

STEP 6 Toolkit Ready
I carry my toolbox of sensory tools to distract my mind and keep me focused on enjoying the flight. They include snacks, my playlists, in-house movies, as well as books and puzzles.

STEP 7 Expect Turbulence (discomfort)
I'm realistic enough to acknowledge that I will experience some form of discomfort throughout the flight. This realism helps reduce any elements of surprise. So, when the turbulence hits, I'm prepared with my anchor and my toolkit to quieten my mind and I can then sit back and enjoy the remainder of the flight.

Ignition Exercise
Facing Your Fear Head On

Now it's your turn to create a simple step-by-step gearbox system to walk through when facing fear head on!

Firstly, name the fear:
_____

STEP 1 Create An Anchor
_____
_____
_____

STEP 2 Test The Anchor
_____
_____
_____

STEP 3 Be Aware Of Mind Jacking
_____
_____
_____
_____

STEP 4 One Step Closer
_____
_____
_____

STEP 5 Embrace The Fear & The Adrenalin Rush

_____
_____
_____

STEP 6 Toolkit Ready

_____
_____
_____

STEP 7 Expect 'Turbulence' (discomfort)

_____
_____
_____
_____

I trust you found the above exercise useful and you're feeling like you have the toolbox and the step-by-step approach to not only face your fears but change gears and drive confidently and seamlessly through the experience.

I'm proud to say that a combination of time, experience and knowledge have diluted my aviophobia. It remains a slight niggle in my mind and a loose knot in my tummy, but I refuse to let it prevent my thirst for adventure and love of travelling.

You have unlimited access to an abundance of energy lying dormant within your own heart and mind. It is such a magical source of all that is wise, loving, timeless and authentic. I encourage you to embrace the unknown, befriend uncertainty and realise the amazing possibilities of driving a life without fear.... a life without limits.

Trip notes

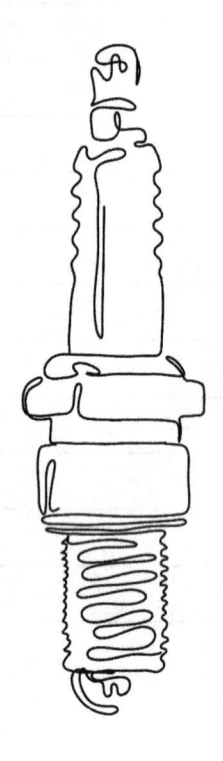

*When you do things from your soul,
you feel a river moving in you.*

RUMI

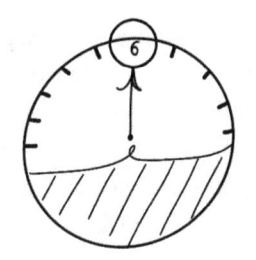

Spark Plugs

Spark Plugs

In November 2017 I made contact with a visionary Swazi named Myxo (Mix-Oh). My sister Donna and I were due to visit Swaziland, South Africa (my birth home), in February the following year, and had eagerly started planning our adventure. I came across Myxo and the travel company he owned while researching tours in Manzini, the second largest urban centre in Swaziland, with a population of approximately 110 000.

Myxo and I started corresponding via email and FaceTime, where it soon became apparent that we shared a passion for children and a love of learning. As I got to know Myxo, I soon realised what he lacked in financial freedom he made up for it in both charm and kindness. I trusted him instantly, his eyes held a gentleness that I could not deny.

My desire to visit an African school had always been a tickle of a thought, but soon developed into a tugging desire. So, as our departure date loomed, I raised the idea with Myxo, who quickly jumped at the opportunity to include a visit to a local rural pre-school in our itinerary. My sister and I finalised our plans for our four day visit to Swaziland, which included an overnight stay in a traditional Swazi village where we would be introduced to their cultural ways, including cooking, conversation, dancing, child rearing and farming.

Days before we flew out of Sydney, bound for Johannesburg and then on to Swaziland, I spent a restless night wondering what gifts I could purchase and pack for the preschool children.
Eventually, I gave up on the hope of sleep, found my laptop and began composing a long email to Myxo.

The blessing of my sleeplessness meant that he was awake on the other side of the world. In the wee small hours of that morning, it was decided that I would spend the next few days raising much needed funds for a water tank for a local rural preschool that we would be visiting.

For the first time in a long time, I felt a roaring fire in my belly, spurred on by the thought of how much joy (as well as water) the gifted tank would bring to the lives of four and five year old Swazi children. Through a GoFund Me account and the generosity of my family and friends, we successfully raised $1325.

Myxo and I spoke excitedly of our plans once my sister and I arrived in Manzini. We had a lot to do. We had a village to provide for!

We arrived by taxi, after a half hour hair raising drive from Mbabane to Manzini. We clocked speeds well over the recommended 120km/hr. As my life flashed past me on the unfamiliar highway, I dared not look sideways at my sister, for fear of nervous giggles escaping.

Our first stop was at the local bustling markets, where a short walk brought us to an outdoor cafe which resembled a clean and simple soup kitchen. Here we were offered a traditional Swazi breakfast, starting with a shared bowl of pap, a traditional porridge made from mielie meal.

My sister and I politely spooned small mouthfuls from the edges of the bowl, whilst having a crash course in Swahili, the native language.

I made phonetic notes on my paper napkin, as Myxo had informed us that we would have an opportunity later in the day to communicate with the locals.

The pap was okay and so was the tea, but the koeksisters (kook-sisters) we shared were even better. Koeksisters are like plaited doughnuts saturated in golden syrup. They seemed an odd choice for breakfast, but we were unsure of when and where our next meal would be, so we happily accepted a second helping. I had enjoyed their sweetness during previous trips I had made to South Africa, when visiting family.

With our bellies full and minds racing with excitement, Myxo drove us through the town towards the hardware store. We had a water tank to source. My sister and I felt a little uneasy, as we were the only white female tourists for miles, my beloved Canon camera blazoned around my neck like a flashing neon tourist sign. As my sister and I ran the few errands with Myxo, we placed our lives in his hands, and I'm sure he sensed this as we tucked in behind him and mirrored his gait.

The village of Kaphunga was well off the beaten track, and at the end of a windy one hour journey into the mountains, we made it to the preschool.
A gathering of mixed aged Swazi women were busy thrashing the long reeds surrounding the quaint rectangular mud schoolhouse. The recent rain had created a red base around the structure, forming a stark contrast with the whitewashed walls.

Myxo introduced us to the teachers and we engaged in polite conversation as they showed us around the bare, single roomed classroom. The pride on their faces reflected their love of the young students, and also of hope for their futures. My smile broadened when I saw a few scattered teaching resources, discarded on the floor. The gaudy plastic seemed ill placed in this rustic space. How indulgent and cluttered my classroom back home now seemed!
Myxo called us outside where, as the only male present, he asked the local ladies to be seated. They dutifully responded, finding a patch of red soil to squat upon. Myxo addressed us all in Swahili and my sister and I smiled and tried to nod our heads intermittently, to feign our understanding of what was being said.

Myxo finished his speech to loud applause from the ladies. Their smiles still cling to me, and their gratitude spoke volumes for their absent words.
A spokeswoman stood and faced us and dug deep to find an English word that carried a similar sentiment to thank you. She paused and smiled and willingly let a short Swahili phrase escape.

I later asked Myxo what she had said and he repeated the Swazi phrase, which when translated meant 'There are no words because of so much gratitude.' Tears of joy pooled in my eyes and I was overcome by a flood of emotions. There were so many lessons that I was learning in that treasured moment and I was trying to catch them all.

These four and five year olds would make the daily five kilometre trek each way to their rural school, unaccompanied by an adult.
Up until now, the children had been asked to carry a litre of water as well as their own water bottles. Once the donated water tank was installed, they wouldn't need to do that! The raw joy I experienced in that moment is something I pause, relive and bathe in regularly. In a poor rural village, a privileged white girl learnt the beauty of human kindness, witnessed the power of human spirit and the beauty of giving and receiving joy from strangers.
We stood as one, as we had received so much from so many.

What Is A Spark Plug?

Spark plugs are tiny bolts of lightning. Small in stature, they are the superheroes under your bonnet. The electricity that they emit creates the combustion that kick starts your ultimate journey. Spark plugs thrive when they are hot and are capable of withstanding extreme pressure.
This should be music to your ears, as it grants you permission to power up and sustain a steady flow of sparks, which will propel you along your journey.

A spark is a passion or a deep interest that lights a fire within a person's soul. Sparks create joy and ignite hope. They reflect a person's character, their values and their dreams, and open windows into the world they want to live in.
A spark is your secret weapon, a motivational tool that requires little effort to fire up and propel you forwards. It assumes many forms, is completely and uniquely personal and is intrinsically treasured.

During Steven Spielberg's Academy of Achievement speech in 2013, he spoke of the notion of having dreams that were sometimes so quiet, they would sneak up on you. Often the spark inside of you is so soft, that it barely whispers its words. However, if you practise allowing enough patience and stillness in your daily life, then you are one step closer to granting the space for the gentle words to dance and the spark to ignite.

Once the spark is ignited, you can expect pure bouts of joy will follow. Now, while we don't exist in a world filled with permanent unicorns and rainbows, nor fireworks and candy clouds, we do live in a world of boundless opportunities and hope. If you can see it in your mind's eye, and feel it in your body, then you can believe it.

Be present in your day, be open to signs from the universe, that she can be trusted to be your guide on this eternal road trip called life.

Sparks are invisible gold which run effortlessly through your veins. They have the power to traverse your body, providing unimaginable joy. For me, that looks like goosebumps and feel like giddy butterflies. Their presence brings me hope and keeps me wanting more! It's what gives me reason to get out of bed each day and brings me closer to living my true purpose.

<u>Finding Your Spark</u>

Most of us have witnessed the magic of people reveling in the joy of their spark. They seem to perform in a hypnotic trance, relishing the freedom and ease of their flow. We have seen teachers, musicians, surgeons, sportswomen and mothers engrossed in their love and their passion. But how do we find our own spark, if we're yet to make its acquaintance?

Ignition Exercise
Playing With Sparks Of Joy

I have posed a handful of questions to prompt your thinking.
Feel free to write down your first thoughts, or take your time and dive deeply. But I'm guessing, if it's your spark you're searching for, it will probably jump up and down, vying for your attention.

1. What was the most recent thing that I did that sparked joy within?

_____
_____
_____

2. What was the most recent thing that I did that gave someone else joy that I was able to witness and experience?

_____
_____
_____

3. What am I curious of and want to know more about?

_____
_____
_____

4. What do I do that I don't label as a chore?

_____
_____
_____

5. What do I look forward to each day or wish that I could do each day?

_____
_____
_____

6. What moves me to tears (happy tears that is)?

_____
_____
_____

7. And for something fun, a question Deborah Hutton, tv presenter and magazine editor posed: "In which section of a bookshop would I happily sleep?"

_____
_____
_____

What Does Your Spark Look Like?

If I were to ask a random group of women what joy looks and feels like to them, I'm almost certain, that there would be an abundance of descriptions.

When I have my spark in front of me or even close to my heart, it feels like goosebumps and I have a grin so wide that sometimes my jaw hurts. My sparks are reflections of hope or recognition on the faces of those people around me. It's almost a cheekiness or guilty pleasure, a temptation to enjoy life's ride alongside the quiet worry of it passing too quickly.

A number of years ago I held a weekend retreat for a group of women aged in their 40s. We were addressing the topic of sparks of joy and reflecting on the one thing that sparks joy in their lives. The women shared their desires openly and honestly.

During this discussion, we referred to the question later used by Marie Kondo: *What sparks joy?* We steered clear of any conversations about rearranged pantries, wardrobes or linen presses. Instead, the women spoke of their dreams; dreams to write children's books, to teach young girls to sew, to open a centre for abused animals, to cycle across Australia, to photograph letterboxes and to raise free range chickens.

The buzz in the room was electric and I wished that I could have bottled the essence of joy and distribute it across the world. These women were alive; their energy mirrored it and their words confirmed it.

My close friend Renai was attending this workshop and her story is worth sharing. I hadn't seen Renai in over a year since that workshop, and out of the blue she messaged me asking if I would like to catch up with her. I jumped at the chance as I always felt relaxed and inspired in her company. I sipped on my coffee at our local cafe, which seemed unusually quiet. I casually looked through the menu while I waited for Renai. I looked up to catch her beaming face walking towards me, a pale cream book tucked under her arm. She looked well and carried a certain sense of achievement in her stride.

I smiled to myself, as she took her seat and spoke excitedly of her morning, her parking spot and how great it was to catch up.

My tribe is deliberately small and hand selected. They nourish me with warmth and kindness. Seated opposite my friend, I could see that she was a reflection of myself and the goodness I also hoped I exuded.

She noticed my eyes land on the book that she had brought with her and like a flood gate bursting under intense pressure, she launched into her exciting news. For the next hour or so, Renai shared with me the moment that she truly recognised her spark, her joy! It was an aha moment and one worthy of a standing ovation! She recalled when it had been her turn during my workshop, to share what sparked joy in her life. I also clearly remembered her speaking of her love of history and especially Asian culture.

"When I had a quiet moment to dissect the emotions I felt during that session of your workshop, I realised something fairly amazing. I had never really let myself feel my spark. I had always read and watched documentaries about Asian history, and I'd always listened to stories about it. In fact, I had been an active bystander of my spark, rather than an active participant in its magic. But having had the opportunity to sit down and share my joy with the ladies present, well that was incredible."

> **I had been an active bystander of my spark, rather than an active participant in its magic.**

Renai went on to tell me that after speaking out aloud about her spark with all of us, she felt that she had finally given herself permission to make visiting China her goal. By unwrapping her spark and revealing its identity, she developed a sense of urgency to fulfil her dream.

Eight months after attending my workshop, Renai and her husband booked their flights to China and tours of the Forbidden City and The Imperial Palace. It was a trip of a lifetime, a dream come true, and proof that true joy lies in wait of your actions.

Now, while overseas adventures may not necessarily be your thing or a viable option, there are simple steps you can take which may lead you to discover your spark within your daily life.

Finding Sparks Of Joy

1. Be present in your day to day life. Befriend silence and seek comfort in its void. Watch its capacity to promote deep, productive thinking.
2. Take time out in nature. Nature has an uncanny way of forcing you to slow down, to be aware and to notice the sparks around you.
3. Practise kindness. The act of kindness is two-fold; in giving joy, you also receive it.

4. Surround yourself with people who see your spark and encourage its power. These people are more likely to be joyful and create positive ripples around you.
5. Compliment someone each day, for what we see in others, is often a reflection of what we see within.
6. Make your bed each morning for no other reason than the joy experienced when you climb into a well made bed, each night.
7. Make contact with someone that you haven't spoken to in a long time.
8. Show gratitude. Once, after a weekend away with my tribe of friends, I decided to write each one of them a letter saying how blessed I felt to have them in my life. The joy of reflecting on the blessing of my tribe was so overwhelming, but an important reminder of how precious friendships are to me.
9. Visit a park and hop on a swing. The giddy feeling in my tummy as I coordinate my legs and body to accelerate me through the air always reminds me of being a child, a time when each day seemed to be filled with insurmountable joy.
10. Smile at those around you, creating a fabulous domino effect. Joy is a contagious emotion which makes us far more attractive and approachable.

Joy vs Happiness

Happiness can be synthesised, artificially manufactured and unfortunately, short lived. Happiness is a more surface levelled emotion which brings pleasure.

Joy on the other hand is a deeper emotion which often lasts for a longer period of time and brings contentment. Joy is triggered by the release of raw emotions and often, indescribably magical.

Along your journey of life, it is usually joy, and not happiness, that will most likely last the distance. So often we are focused on chasing happiness that we may overlook the simplicity of joy. When we look for opportunities to experience and create joy, we build our emotional resilience and enjoy the drive. This helps prepare us to face any potholes, detours, speed bumps and breakdowns along the way.

Be sure to catch the random and intangible moments of joy which you may encounter on your travels. These may reveal themselves in the form of smiles, waves, handshakes and random acts of kindness. Joy may manifest in the most incredible ways.

Tickles Of Joy

Children bring me the most amount of joy. They are round, colourful vessels of fun. They are messy, playful and unpredictable. Children are crazy contradictions of curiosity and challenges. I left teaching almost 10 years ago at the right time. Working with children brought me joy daily, but the politics and rules governing my environment were making me increasingly unhappy. I knew that I could no longer sustain my enthusiasm and inevitably, the children were bound to feel the growing wrath of my discontentment.

So, I made the brave decision to listen to the tickle that Steven Spielberg talks about and I closed the door on a successful teaching career. I say *brave* now, but at the time it was out of necessity rather than courage, that I took the leap of faith. Obviously, other factors were considered by my husband and I, predominantly around financial viability and what the next step would look like for us.

At the time, I was naively unsure of the financial side of things and I just wanted to remain in my bubble of sweet ignorance. But seriously, I knew that the universe would take care of me, she always did and continues to. I was educated, healthy and positive, which allowed me to hold the key to spark the ignition of my next journey.

We relied on our savings and my reputation to build a small tutoring business, which has now grown into a business which I'm so passionate about and one which brings me untold joy.
Were there tough times? You bet!
Did I steer off course a few times? Absolutely!
Did I suffer from blurred vision and blind spots? Definitely.
Did I ever look back in the rear view mirror of regrets? Not once!

Ignition Exercise
What Sparks Joy For You?

What is the one thing in your life which brings you joy? What is the joy that combusts in your belly; the joy that is often unexplainable with words and best felt in the body?

Cast your mind back to the Heart space in the chapter on goals, where you allowed yourself to freely dream. What is the tickle or whisper inside of you that is begging for an audition, its five minutes of fame? Acknowledge it for what it is and what it represents, without the fogginess of doubt, judgment or exclusion.

I give you permission to release your spark and let it skip across the lines below. Be curious and for goodness sake, drink in the magic!

What sparks joy within you?

_____
_____
_____

<u>Jump Start Joy</u>

There are speed bumps and potholes throughout all of our journeys. There will be times when your battery will be flat and you will struggle to find the motivation to go on. This is when you may need to pull over, reconnect with your values, your goals and just breathe. Sit on the side of the road and soak up the view. Listen to your intuition, it will know how to reset your GPS and make a new plan.

Remind yourself of the spark that brings you joy, what inspires you to wake up with a purpose each day. Have a word, a phrase, a feeling! What is your spark that lights up your world and gives you a reason to get out of bed?

At the end of the day, remember that life is a great balancing act, requiring an equal blend of work, rest and play. Sometimes your spark sits right beneath your nose, politely waiting to be sniffed out. It may be disguised as a tickle, gathering its confidence to become a tug. Regardless, remember that your spark is your passion and something you willingly commit to. You rarely need to be reminded to enjoy it nor forced to embrace it.

Spark plugs are vital to your Kombi's efficiency and hold the key to a smooth and responsive journey. When we're firing on all cylinders, our mind and body are in sync and we are functioning at our optimal potential. When you know what sparks joy within, you are one step closer to realising your purpose and mapping out your journey. Congratulations!

Your driver's seat is comfy, your windscreen is clear, your baggage is stowed and your brakes are released. Your spark plugs are firing and your GPS is set. Time to grab hold of the steering wheel, to feel the power of responsibility and being in control.

Remember, it's impossible to steer a parked Kombi, so be on your way!

Trip notes

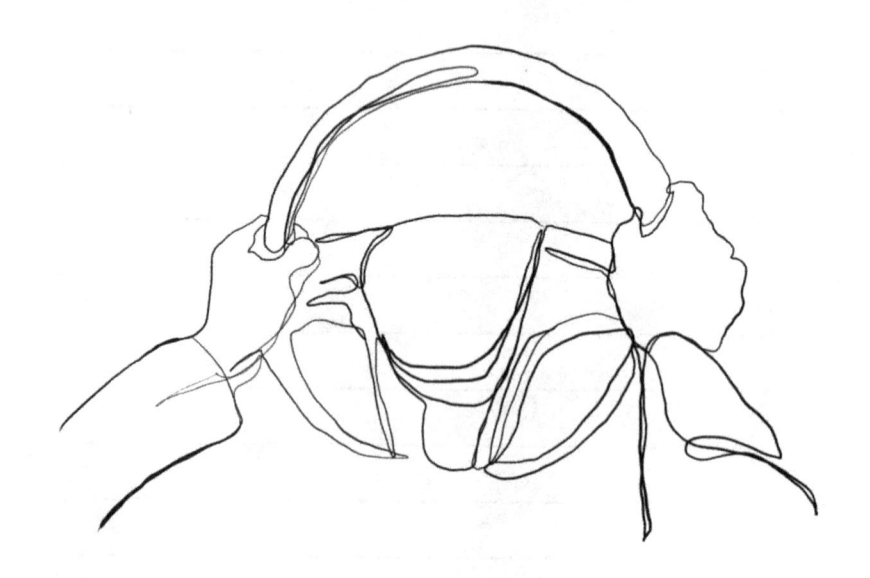

*Choose a job you love,
and you will never have to work
a day in your life.*

CONFUCIUS

The Steering Wheel

The Steering Wheel

The light drizzle did very little to dampen my anticipation. I made my way across the empty schoolyard and couldn't help but notice the barren red soil, a stark contrast to the vanilla walls of the basic schoolhouse that stretched out around me. The simple yet effective roofing provided relief from the persistent rain, but the temporary guttering sagged crudely, buckling under the weight of the collected water.

Our guide, Myxo, directed us to a particular classroom, one of three which stood together in a neat row. We waited patiently outside Mr Alex's classroom door.
I had met with him the evening prior, where we engaged in polite conversation about teaching and children, and everything in between.

I remember agreeing to disagree on one particular topic which highlighted the vastness which suspended our two cultures. He had said to me that he would never reveal to his students when he was uncertain of an answer or unsure of an explanation. He went on to justify that his students would judge his lack of knowledge and view him as inadequate, incompetent and would no doubt, disrespect him as an educator.
I retorted by sharing that I openly tell my students when I lack the ability or understanding to confidently respond to their questions. Instead, I encourage them to take the initiative to explore the answers themselves and to then enlighten me with their findings. I gently reminded him, that we are all life-long learners who have the capacity to initiate and explore the fountain of knowledge, for our own personal growth and enrichment.

As a teacher and parent, I believe that while I draw breath, I learn. I learn from life experiences, from the children I work with, the books I devour and from a wealth of many other sources. I am a curious human being. I simply thrive on the acquisition of new knowledge and the opportunity to share what I learn with others.

I glanced through the slightly ajar door of the busy classroom to see a scuffed concrete floor, an extension of the path that we were standing upon. Restless feet attached to worn out shoes fidgeted as the outline of their teacher drew closer towards us. Mr Alex appeared in the doorway, a tall athletic man blessed with a youthful face and a strong physique.

He invited us into a sea of beaming smiles from curious children, happy with the unfolding distraction I had created. I paused to catch my breath and the enormity of this situation, which seemed to be propelling at full speed and I was being swept along, totally bewildered. I scanned the room like I often did when experiencing a magical moment such as this, I drank in the emotions and let my senses loose to play with the euphoria.

I awkwardly took my place in front of the green chalkboard which almost spanned the length of one wall. Perfectly structured cursive sentences flowed across the board, obviously waiting to be recorded in the students' exercise books, which lay upon their desks. There were eyes everywhere, all fixed upon me. I had dreamed of this moment since forever.

Surprisingly, I felt nervous and I tried desperately to tame the butterflies building residence within. The children sat in perfectly arranged rows, in a blur of mixed sized blue school uniforms.

Teaching in an African school had always been a pipe dream, a bucket list experience, combining my South African heritage and my love of teaching.
This moment seemed so surreal yet so perfect.

I honestly can't recall the words of hopeful wisdom that escaped my mouth but it brought laughter and incredible energy within the four walls. Coincidently, and lucky for me, the students had been engaged in a geography lesson prior to my arrival. Thinking quickly on my feet, and desperate to bridge a connection through the cultural barriers, I decided to refer the students to the world map in the centre pages of their atlases. This paid off and the children were able to use their fingers to trace the flight path I had travelled from Australia to South Africa. Laughter broke out again amongst the students when Mr Alex said that the flight would have taken at least half a day.

My visit lasted twenty minutes or so and I then handed out my gifts to Mr Alex - koala and kangaroo key rings. I mimicked the actions of a kangaroo, to which they laughed with me, which eased my awkwardness. I longed for more time with them, I had just found my groove. Mr Alex asked me to record the words koala and kangaroo upon the chalkboard to which they dutifully practised their pronunciations.

As I stood in front of these curiously respondent children, I realised something very profound! I felt it then and I still feel it now. My purpose in life is to nurture young minds; it's what brings me joy. I truly believe the world benefits indirectly from my gifts, but more so from my passion.

Writer and theologian, Frederick Buechner, suggests that your purpose lies at the intersection of your greatest joy and the world's greatest need. For me, standing before the sea of eager eyes and curious minds in the classroom in Swaziland, I realised this exact notion. I stood in a deliciously joyful space, immersed in the purest form of contentment, willfully educating them, yet being taught by them. In that moment, I was at the junction where my passion for kindness met my purpose of empowering children and my dream of teaching the children of Africa.

Whilst I no longer teach within the confines of a classroom, I can say with honesty, that each day I am living my purpose. We have many choices offered to us every day and to move towards our purpose we need to steer our life in the direction we want to go.

The steering wheel is the control arm of your Kombi. It is the spokesperson of the steering system, the first responder to your actions as a driver. The steering wheel awaits your instruction and willingly transmits messages to the wheels to start moving. Your Kombi needs traction to get you on your way, and once you know the purpose of your journey, the last thing left to do is grab the steering wheel and go!

When seated comfortably in your driver's seat, behind the steering wheel of your Kombi, your journey is destined to be self-determined and self-driven.
You should feel reassured that you have almost completed the initial stages of preparations for the trip and completed your vehicle checks.

Through careful consideration of your values, your goals, your fears, your baggage and your dreams, you are one step closer to steering yourself in any direction you choose.

Like with any journey, knowing the general direction of your travels is mandatory, to steer towards either a programmed destination or the first steps in an unfolding adventure.

What Does Purpose Mean?

Purpose is defined as the reason behind what you do, how you do it and why you do what you do. Your sense of purpose steers how you want the story of your life to go. Behind any successful life narrative is a practical framework, steering your flow of thoughts towards an inevitable and purposeful conclusion.

Knowing your purpose provides you with the reservoir through which you can filter your decisions to determine whether your actions are in alignment with your values and your priorities. Your purpose should complement your passion (curiosity), your gifts and your skills. Your purpose in life is, in essence, your steering wheel to guide your Kombi towards your destination.

I feel fortunate to have discovered my purpose at a young age. Maybe it was by chance or by circumstance but nonetheless, I knew at the age of 18 that I wanted to be a teacher. However, at the age of 15, I thought very differently and had high aspirations of becoming a professional dancer.

At the time, I was a Year 10 student and able to apply for work experience within any suitable industry or workplace of my choice. I excitedly met with the school's ageing career's advisor, who I was certain had a calendar behind her office door secretly marking off the days towards her retirement.
I begged her (well politely asked her), to approach Sydney Dance Company and request that I participate in one week's work experience with them. After all, I was a talented ballerina, a supple acrobat and had the dedication of an intrepid explorer.

My application was successful, and I was even granted special conditions to complete the experience outside of the school's scheduled time frame.
I remember arriving at the contemporary studios nestled amongst Sydney's historic foreshore. It was a unique space which intimidated me from the start.
I casually carried my dance bag over one shoulder, being sure to catch a glimpse of my reflection before I entered the reception area.

I prayed that I looked cool enough as I adjusted my posture to mirror the dancers who gracefully sashayed ahead of me. I received an information package from the receptionist who kindly directed me to the rehearsal studio at the end of the long corridor, for the morning warm up.

I sat alone on the concrete floor, fiddling awkwardly with my ballet ribbons, stalling for time and trying to avoid the curious glances by the company's dancers. In hindsight, this exact moment may have been when I realised that my purpose was not to dance! I feel like it was more than just the pity filled faces of the dancers that helped me reach this conclusion. I just knew it. I was young but not delusional.

There was no doubt I had talent, perhaps a small gift, but definitely not a God given purpose! I endured the grueling twenty minute warm up, well only just!

I was relieved when the pianist stopped and the trainer approached me and quietly explained that the warm up was finished and that I could head to reception for further instruction. That was the first and last class I attended during my week at the Company.

The remainder of the time I spent answering phones, hemming the dancers' rehearsal skirts and typing cheques. I couldn't have chosen three more awkward tasks to retract deeper into my shell. I had never hemmed a skirt nor typed a cheque and answering telephones was almost as painful for me as the class I had just endured!

While reminiscing about this experience at the innocent age of fifteen makes me cringe, it forced me to quickly reconsider my options post Year 12. For this was a time where my talent alone could not support my purpose. My steering was out of alignment, and the discomfort and instability I experienced, reaffirmed that for me.

Ignition Exercise

Does Your Steering Need Re-alignment?

Are you able to recall an experience which sent a very loud message to you that you were out of your depth and quickly sinking? Was there a time where perhaps your talent and skills set were out of alignment with your passion? Did it result in extreme embarrassment, like in my situation?
Or are you still 'hemming the skirts' of other peoples' achievements?

_____
_____
_____
_____
_____

Now that you have acknowledged what your purpose isn't or wasn't, let me help steer you towards finding your true purpose.

How Do I Find My Purpose?

For the past thirty years, I have been following my purpose of teaching. While the teaching environment had changed a little throughout my career, my focus remained clear, and my spark had stayed relatively charged. That was until I ventured off course and started to steer towards a place where I felt discomfort and despair.

Teaching had changed, or maybe it was me who had changed. My classroom became my cage where I found no escape. I was trapped by the binds of mandatory curriculum, predictive lessons and generic reporting. I had reached burnout and my spark was more than snuffed, it was forcibly extinguished. The darkness of my faintly smoldering spark could no longer steer me on.

I slammed on the brakes, let go of the steering wheel and ejected from the driver's seat. I left teaching that same year and I have never looked back. Despite this tumultuous time in my life, I was relieved that my purpose to empower children remained strong and that it became my pillar of strength to lean on.

Ten years on, I have my own successful coaching and tuition business which I run from my studio at home. I am following my purpose, fueling my passion, utilising my gifts and applying my skills set. I wake up each day with a purpose which allows me to continue to teach with passion and to empower children. I have devised an equation for my life's purpose and it flows like so:

<u>THE PASSION-TO-PURPOSE SYSTEM</u>
passion + gift + skill = purpose

My passion is children, my gift is patience and my skill is teaching, hence I am living a purposeful life by empowering children to become confident and resilient life-long learners.

Here are some helpful questions and tips to steer you towards your purpose.

<u>What Is My Passion Or What Sparks My Curiosity?</u>

You may wish to revisit Chapter 6 on Spark Plugs as pre-reading for this chapter. Remember, that sometimes your spark or passion sits right beneath your nose, politely waiting to be sniffed out. For some people, it's disguised as a tickle, while for some it's screaming out for attention. Regardless, remember that your spark is your passion and something you willingly commit to. When engrossed in your passion or something that you are curious about, you rarely need to be reminded to enjoy it, nor forced to embrace it.

Your curiosity is a key driver in steering you towards personal success. If you have ever hung out with a four-year-old, you will know that they are naturally curious bubbles of infinite questions. They have successfully mastered the never-ending string of *whys?*

Jon Cohen, chief research officer of Survey Monkey, reports that on average, four year olds ask up to 300 questions each day. Sadly, by the time some children reach adolescence, their thirst for knowledge is somewhat tamed and their curiosity may become effected by social influences such as peer judgement.

The curse of teenage apathy - and possibly from repetitious comments made by adults like, "Just because" or "Don't question me!" - may be responsible for their depleted curiosity. Thankfully, by the time we reach our early 20s, we tend to resurface from the depths of *'whatever'* take a gulp of fresh air, and get curious again in our new surroundings.

Most of us are curious creatures who eagerly question life and what it has to offer, while some people accept almost everything at face value. Similarly, some of us are happy to climb on board our Kombis and willingly grasp the steering and trust that it knows the way.

Ignition Exercise
What Is My Passion?
What Steers My Curiosity?

<u>What Is My Gift?</u>

The famous Spanish artist Pablo Picasso suggested that the meaning of life is to find your gift and then the purpose of life is to give it away. So, to provide you with clarity around your purpose, perhaps you could identify the gifts that you have?
By definition, your gifts are your innate, unique talents which come naturally. Your gift may look like empathy, feel like connection and sound like leadership.
It may announce itself during childhood or patiently wait for the onset of adulthood or midway through life.

Not everyone comes into their gift easily or naturally. Regardless, we are all bestowed with gifts and they are there to be shared.

GIFTS: What are my gifts?

_____

_____

Jearlyn Steele, American singer, speaker & TV host, poses an interesting question, which I encourage you to respond to below.
What is something that you would do if you were never paid for it?

_____

_____

Steve Harvey, author and comedian, believes that by following your gifts, you will enjoy a wonderful career, a career which you are paid for. Your calling is what you were made for. Your calling and your gift are the two ends of a ribbon, eagerly anticipating entwinement to become one.

What Are My Skills?

Your skillset is the combination of knowledge, abilities and personal qualities that you have developed through your experiences in life and work.

Your skills may include interpersonal skills; including impressive communication, active listening, emotional prowess, or attention to detail.

SKILLS: What are my skills?

_____

_____

Hang Out With People Who Are Following Their Purpose

Listen to podcasts, read biographies, attend talks, just do whatever it takes to steer you into the minds and hearts of people who are living their purpose.
Be curious about how they found their purpose and what they are doing each day to live by it.

I recall listening to Elizabeth Gilbert, well known author of *Eat, Pray, Love* deliver a most inspiring talk on how she discovered her love of writing.
I distinctively remember her advice to us novice authors in the audience, on how to avoid overwhelm when writing. She suggested that authors should have one person in mind, for whom they are writing their book. If at the end of the writing process, that one person is the only one who reads a gifted or purchased copy of your book, then the writing journey has been a success.

For me, to hear Elizabeth speak not only of her passion but how she has turned her gift into her purpose, inspired me enormously. So much so, that as I have steered my way through the writing of this book, I have kept one person in mind who I would love to be the first to read it.
That gives me hope, holds my focus and keeps the steering locked on my purpose to potentially make a difference in the lives of women!

Ignition Exercise
...at Is Following Their Purpose and Passion?

Think of someone who is engaged in a career, an area of interest, a passion that is similar to yours (and appears to be enjoying it).

_____

_____

How do you know that they are enjoying their pursuit?

_____
_____
_____

What are they doing that shows that they are enjoying their passion, following their purpose, or exploring their curiosity?

_____
_____

<u>Say Yes</u>

One of the best pieces of advice that I was given about finding my purpose was imparted on me when studying my Certificate IV in Life Coaching in 2011. Before my training, I will happily admit that I was a people pleaser, part of the perfection routine I was performing. I would go out of my way to do and say things to please everybody, even to the detriment of my own happiness.

Like the child struggling for friends, offering to buy attention with canteen treats, I wanted to be liked, so I assumed the people pleaser role. It was exhausting and unsustainable. It wasn't until I hit my late 40s that I gained clarity around my need to always say *Yes*.

I needed to redefine my belief systems around the relationship between the word *Yes*, meaning growth, as opposed to *Yes* meaning people pleasing.

The growth that being committed to Yes brings, includes new opportunities, new vision and perhaps a change in my steering direction. Wisdom and experience have helped me to realise that when presented with an opportunity, it can either strengthen the steering direction of my travels or complete a significant reprograming of my GPS.

There are a few questions I carefully need to consider before I say YES. Will saying "Yes" -

1. Challenge me and encourage personal growth?
2. Align with my values and vision?
3. Inspire those around me?
4. Steer me closer towards finding my purpose?

How Do I Live My Purpose?

Now that you have identified your gift, your skills and your spark, you need to get creative and figure out how you can build your purpose around the source of your joy.

I have sat through enough eulogies to bear witness to some common threads. Most family and friends speak with specially crafted words, which serve to celebrate the life of those who have passed. Heartfelt words capture memories of meaningful lives lived well and lifelong dreams devoured. However, more often than not, the recollections of how the lives of those still living were enhanced by the deceased, is what echoes long after the curtains are closed and the final handful of dust is thrown.

In researching material for this chapter, I asked a number of people a selection of questions. I have tried to include a diverse range of responses from women of all ages, including some who have found their purpose as well as those who are still searching. I admire their courage, tenacity and willingness to share their responses.

Below are the questions I asked:
1. What are you curious/passionate about?
2. What are your skills and your gifts?
3. Who or what benefits from your passion, skills and gifts?
4. a) What is your current employment?
   b) How does what you're currently doing steer you towards your purpose?

As you can see, I kept the questions simple, specific and closed. The table below provides a sample of some of the results. It's a useful example of how your purpose may reveal itself simply by steering towards curiosity and passion.

What are you curious/ passionate about?	What are your gifts?	What are your skills?	Who or what benefits from your passions, skills and gifts?	What is your current employment?	How does what you're currently doing steer you towards your purpose?
Helping animals JESS 18	Connection with animals, particularly horses	Ability to communicate with horses and build trust	Myself & animals	Working at a horse rehab centre	I don't know what I want to do with my life yet but where I am right now is perfect for the time being as I'm doing something I love and that I am passionate about.
Hair & empowering women KYLIE 34	Artistic ability and human connection	Hair colouring Cutting, Upstyling	My family and my friends	Hairdresser and hair salon owner	I love being part of a community and feeling a sense of contribution which tells me that I'm living my purpose.
Making a difference in the lives of others CATHY 40+	Patience, Empathy	Listening, Communication, Honest & Hardworking Organisation skills	The children and young adults who I work with. My colleagues My family & friends	Administrator at a school for students on the Autism Spectrum.	I feel that what I am currently doing is in alignment to some extent but could be better aligned.
Helping others, Women's rights, The Earth, Women birthing, Animal rights JODIE 40+	Empathy, Human connection, Generosity	Listening, Communication, Conversation	My family My friends My meditation/ yoga students Strangers	Yoga & meditation teacher	Sure does!

Now it's your turn!

What are you curious/ passionate about?	What are your gifts?	What are your skills?	Who or what benefits from your passions, skills and gifts?	What is your current employment?	How does what you're currently doing steer you towards your purpose?

Realising and Embracing Your Road Map

Hopefully, you now have some clarity around your purpose, or at least know what you're curious about pursuing and have some ideas of how to steer towards it. I have designed a task to throw yourself into and most importantly, to have fun doing.

All you'll need is a blank piece of paper and some pens, markers, pencils and an open mind. For the creative souls out there, you can drag out your leftover scrapbooking bits and pieces and bedazzle it a little or a lot. This will be a work in progress, with additions, eliminations and some things 'to be continued'.

This exercise is all about you; your destination, your goal, your purpose.
First, I would like to share a story, which I believe best illustrates the value of this task. I will use my best friend Paul as an example.

After carefully considering the Passion-to-Purpose System that I detailed earlier in the chapter, I began talking to Paul about his passion and purpose. He immediately identified working with animals as his passion. His gifts are his empathetic nature, his curiosity, his patience and gentleness amongst other admirable traits. His skillset includes being a practical and hands on learner.
The animals he cares for are the obvious benefactors of his combined passion, gifts and skills. As he is currently on a working visa, enjoying his third year in Australia, he is engaged in rural work at a local orchard. While fruit picking, crop preparation, pruning and bottling of juice is a means to an end, he's well aware that it's fairly removed from what he is most passionate about – animals.

While completing his first year working visa requirements, he was employed in a battery chicken shed for close to three months, collecting eggs and retrieving deceased hens. This was a direct contradiction of his ethical stance on animal treatment. However, to extend his stay in our country, he had to do what he had to do. While the monotony of the work numbed his emotional pain, at the end of each day he knew that he was another day closer to moving on.

His time spent in the chicken shed could have been soul crushing; but instead, it built his resilience and fueled his passion to rescue animals and build safe, expansive environments for them to flourish.

Sometimes we can plummet into overwhelm when our vision becomes too expansive, and our expectations are set too high. I'm an advocate for making small steps a big priority rather than big steps a small priority. The diagram below depicts Paul's road map and shows the small steps he has taken in living his purpose.

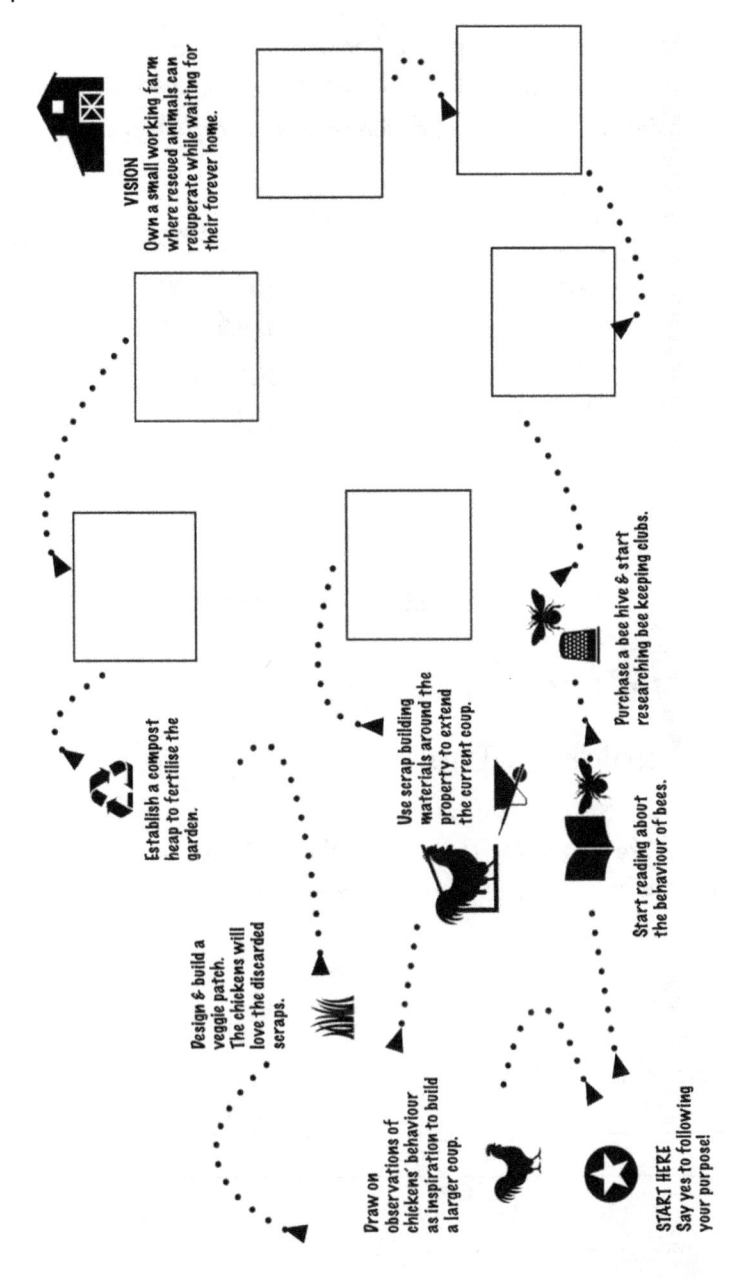

VISION
Own a small working farm where rescued animals can recuperate while waiting for their forever home.

Establish a compost heap to fertilise the garden.

Design & build a veggie patch. The chickens will love the discarded scraps.

Use scrap building materials around the property to extend the current coup.

Purchase a bee hive & start researching bee keeping clubs.

Start reading about the behaviour of bees.

Draw on observations of chickens' behaviour as inspiration to build a larger coup.

START HERE
Say yes to following your purpose!

Ignition Exercise
Design Your Road Map

Please feel free to use Paul's road map as guidance and inspiration to complete your own, on a separate piece of paper. Remember to include the little steps, the leaps, the side steps and importantly the backward steps. Every step is a form of action and is moving you closer towards the realisation of your purpose.

Your passion, your gifts, your skillset and your curiosity, are the rods which make up the steering system and there for you to utilise as you move towards your purpose. They are there to help you steer towards something as well as the reason why you will steer away from it.

> **Your passion, your gifts, your skillset and your curiosity, are the rods which make up the steering system.**

Ignition Exercise
Exploring The Why

The author of *Chicken Soup for The Soul* books, Jack Canfield, suggests that in order to clarify your purpose you should know what the *why* is behind everything you do.

By asking yourself:

What makes me come alive? And Why?

_____

_____

What sparks joy? And Why?

_____
_____
_____

What do I do that is effortless? And Why?

_____
_____
_____

What can I do that will be of benefit to others? And Why?

_____
_____

And lastly, feel free to complete your own Passion to Purpose equation. I have included mine as well as Paul's as an example.

Passion + gift + skill = purpose

Children + patience + teaching = empowering children

Animals + empathy + practicality = caring for animals

Now it's your turn!

_____

In answering these questions and completing your own Passion to Purpose equation, you will hopefully steer closer towards your purpose and perhaps even notice the ease of your grip on the steering wheel!

Trip notes

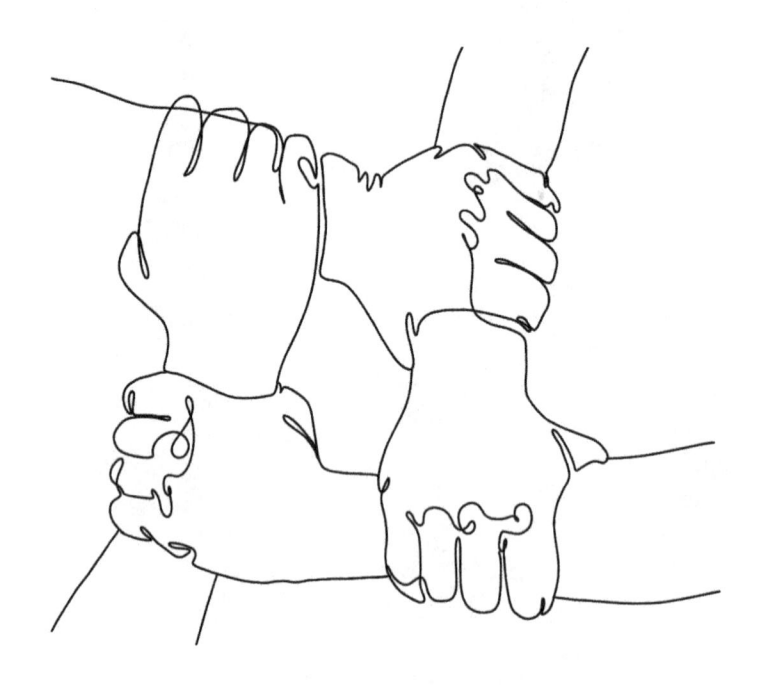

Be slow to fall in to friendship; but when thou art in, continue firm and constant.

SOCRATES

The Passengers

The Passengers

We had been planning our seaside getaway for months, trying to find a weekend which suited all six of us. Without really needing a reason why, we pencilled in the chosen date in October, which fortunately for me, coincided with my birthday.

We had found the perfect accommodation, which ticked all the boxes including the pièce de résistance, impressive sprawling ocean views. The modern split-level home was an architect's delight. It politely nestled itself along the Pacific coastline, commanding a front row seat to the vast expanse.

In preparing for our trip, we decided that we would each bring a selection of food to place into a communal pantry and fridge and 'make it work'. Knowing my tribe, I felt confident that this would involve baskets of ripe fruit and vegetables, freshly baked breads and muffins, bottles of boutique wines and an abundance of chocolate treats. We always enjoyed good food and never took shortcuts.

Supermarket visits were definitely banned during this getaway. Instead, we were to rely on one another to carefully choose produce which would suit all dietary needs and sustain long lunches, accompany pre-dinner drinks and compliment the sweet teeth amongst us!

And my tribe didn't let me down. I must admit, the unpacking of all our delights was one of the highlights of our weekend, so much so that the event was celebrated with the obligatory fluted bubbles and finely dressed platters of cheese and biscuits. We must have stood in the kitchen for hours, taste testing the food and enjoying the deliciousness of the time that passed.

The following evening, my self-confessed hippie-dippie friend, Jodie, asked us all to be seated around the dining room table. There was a gentle light which danced around the room, forcing us to focus on the candle she held lovingly in her hand.

Jodie addressed us with her familiar relaxed confidence; her rich tones always seem to sooth my soul and send me into a hypnotic trance. In between her considered pauses, I stole a glance around the table and smiled knowing that I was quite possibly the luckiest girl in the world. Seated before me, was my tribe. These people, next to my family, were the ones I loved and entrusted with my life.

To commence our sacred ceremony, Jodie asked us to take it in turns to use her beacon of light to ignite the individual bees' wax candles, positioned in front of us. We allowed the silence to envelop us, and surrendered to its magic. The ethereal glow from the outstretched table held our collective breath and suppressed any unsaid words.

Sensing the deliciousness of this unexpected experience, Jodie held the space and gently broke the moment when she sensed it time. She then asked each member to take out the beads that they had been asked to bring along with them. (She is always so organised when it comes to matters of the heart).

She explained to the tribe (excluding me), that as the thread of elastic was passed around the table, each member would take it in turns to hold their bead/s and share a story of how they met me, as well as what they love and admire about me. I watched as my tribe passed the threaded beads from friend to friend, witnessing the compilation of my treasured keepsake.

The placement of each bead on the elastic was accompanied by a birthday blessing from my tribe member, including their dreams and hopes for my future. When it was Jodie's turn, she secured a quaint silver charm amongst the other beads. The goddess of Tiki represented the inner strength of feminine energy and I was thrilled to have her included in my tribal keepsake.

I have never and perhaps will never again, experience such a self-indulgent moment. As I sat and listened to the deepest articulations of the most heartfelt and honest words, I prayed for time to slow down to walking pace, so that I could catch up. The rich qualities that I have worked so hard to nurture internally, and to share externally, were being reflected back at me and I was proud. I was proud of the woman I was becoming, the shell of the woman I had released and the women I would go forth to inspire. Although I was many kilometres from my family, I felt like the comfort of home had climbed into my heart, hugged me and softly whispered "You're home."

That was the moment I understood the meaning of having a tribe and acknowledging the rarity of such a find. My tribe are my white peacocks, my hidden gems. They are my north, my east, my south and my west.

My tribe help me navigate this life, making my journey an adventurous and fulfilling one!

> **My tribe are my white peacocks, my hidden gems.**

What Are Passengers?

Passengers are the people who are aboard your Kombi. They are the passengers in your life journey, there for your enjoyment (and hopefully their own). They are either there by invitation, mutual selection or somehow they have jumped onboard, along your trip. Either way, you are the driver of your Kombi and you can decide who you allow on, who can stay, and who needs to disembark at the next stop.

Your passengers are your confidants, the friends you seek honest advice from and refer to as extended family. They are your collective safe house of warmth, acceptance and generosity of spirit. Your passengers are the chosen ones you effortlessly share your time and energy with, to fuel the tribal flame which burns brightly.

As you work through this chapter, trust that the passengers you end up hand selecting to ride this journey with you may be there for a reason, a season or a lifetime. And that's okay. As we are forever evolving and changing, so too are our friendships. And that's also okay.

Long Term Friendships

I recently caught up for a long overdue coffee with a friend who has been in my life for the past 13 years. We don't live in each other's pockets, but we share a mutual understanding that we are there for each other, no matter what.

We sipped our coffee and nibbled on the last few crumbs of our carrot cake. We took it in turns to bring each other up to speed with news of our families, our work and travels. An easy hour passed. She then posed an interesting question, which provided considerable material for this chapter of my book.

"Do you have any close, long-term friends?" she finally asked me. Being careful not to race into my response, I hovered above it for a moment and thought carefully about my answer. Firstly, I clarified what she meant by *long term* and she said that she felt it included friendships spanning more than twenty years.

With that in mind, I spoke of my longest standing friends who easily fit into her predetermined category. They were initially friends for a reason (school days, teaching days and dancing days) but all have become lifetime friends. My response led to the relatively quick peeling back of several more layers of our conversation, which got deep very quickly. I started to ask myself the big questions.

How are friendships formed?

What is the initial spark that captures your interest and holds your attention when it comes to friends?

What are the qualities or values you seek in your passengers?

My answer was universal to all of these questions. For me it simply was one word - connection! Connection has sustained my longest friendships, spanning over 30 plus years.

The Magic Of Connection

Connection to me is a special feeling; an intimate bond between two souls often requiring minimal conversation yet resulting in undeniable vibes. Connections are as rare as they are addictive, as moorish as they are treasured. I recently came across my musings on connection in a journal I kept in 2018.

> *Connection is like bottled perfection.*
> *Rich in colour, yet transparent in simplicity.*
> *It is beautifully warm and addictive in nature,*
> *leaving us wanting more.*
> *Connections are timeless, yet instant in time.*
> *They conjure internal excitement with vibrant bubbles*
> *of possibilities.*
> *I love the feeling of connection and the joy in its randomness.*
> *They offer everything and demand nothing.*
> *They are purely there to be felt, nurtured and treasured.*
> *Connections are beyond explanation for someone's judgement,*
> *but more about self enjoyment and indulgence.*

I want to feel the magic of connection with all my passengers, and I encourage you to want that as well. Be open to change and flexible in your choices.
Your journey is yours to drive and you obviously want to have fun along the way. So, choose your passengers wisely, you at least deserve that privilege. For the purpose of this chapter, I will refer to my passengers as my tribe, for they are my closest friends and the souls who hold my hands and my heart.

What Is A Tribe?

At the seasoned age of 51, I feel that I have earned the right to my own definition of a tribe. For me, a tribe is a collection of like-minded souls who share an unexplainable connection and a steely bond, strengthened by common values, embraced in a protective forcefield.
It's typically a smallish group with common interests, values, vision and purpose.
The obvious yet unspoken bond of a tribe seems to provide a safety net to ensure its' members survival, through life's speed bumps and obstacles; life's sharp twists and turns. Friendships seem to come and go, like the phases of the moon, but belonging to a tribe offers another layer of goodness for the soul.

A tribe provides a stable platform for your authentic self to shine; a stage for you to receive standing ovations, and lots of them. As passengers, your tribe affords the support system and stability of your Kombi. They keep the driver entertained, calm and focused on the journey.

Your Vibe Attracts Your Tribe

The common threads of interest form the fabric of your tribe and cocoon you in its protective warmth. For me, I have enjoyed the company of the same tribe for the past 6 or so years, along this road trip that I call life. They have been there for me through the bumps, blind spots and detours.

They were my reliable pit crew throughout my 'midlife cleanse' which saw me dealing with a multitude of raw emotions.
They held front row seats as I walked away from my teaching career and watched from the sidelines as I established my coaching business.

> **The common threads of interest form the fabric of your tribe and cocoon you in its protective warmth.**

My tribe were the wind which shifted the fog, cleared the confusion and held the space for me to recalculate my journey.

I know that I have found my tribe; I know that I have earned the right to be choosey. My tribe sparks joy in many facets of my life. They inspire me to be the best version of me, they motivate me to challenge myself, but importantly, they reflect the reservoir of goodness that I have stored in my engine.

They grant me unspoken permission to be my true self and carry my hopes in their silent prayers and wishes. To be passengers in my Kombi, I need a tribe who are heading in the same direction as myself. Their vision may differ, depending on the view from the seat they sit upon, but I see that as having very little impact on the vibe within the Kombi. If anything, it will only enhance the mood and energy.

If I was to run my eye over my tribe as they prepared themselves to find their seat aboard my Kombi, they would share six common traits. My tribe possess a combination of the following qualities, which I value and honour.

My tribe are:
1. Kind
2. Curious
3. Grateful
4. Open minded
5. Dreamers
6. Adventurous

Tribal Member Qualities

I'm a sucker for kindness. Therefore, it is the most important quality that I'm drawn to as a prerequisite for my tribal members. If I was to ask my passengers which value is in their top three, I'm almost certain that kindness would resonate amongst them.

Ignition Exercise
Qualities Of Your Tribe

You may already be blessed with your own precious passengers, or you may be slowly gathering them. Whatever the case, I would like you to think about the qualities of your ideal passenger in your Kombi. Make a list of all the traits that your ideal passenger will possess. Remember that in order to attract your ideal passengers, you need to be projecting what you are seeking. After all, your vibe attracts your tribe.

For example, if you are drawn to qualities such as warmth and kindness, then you need to be modelling those characteristics in your own behaviour. Otherwise, you'll end up driving solo, without passengers to help share in your adventures.

_____

_____

_____

_____

Keep in mind that your passengers are able to indulge in flexible seating plans. Depending on your moods and certain situations that you may find yourself in, you may need to shuffle your passengers' seats around.

You may choose a particular friend to ride shot gun next to you, so you can talk it out quietly, side by side without involving the whole tribe. Or there may be times when you require an abundance of support, which may see you join your tribe in the back seat of your Kombi while you let someone else drive.

Responsibilities As The Driver Of My Passengers

As the driver of my passengers, I am always reminded of the gifts that they bring with them and the value they add to my journey. With any membership of a club or organisation, comes expectations and responsibilities. My passengers need to feel that they are appreciated and that their time and energy are well invested! I'll be the first to admit that I don't devote nearly enough time to phone calls or FaceTime catchups. But I'm sure that my passengers would attest that in person, I am present, generous and one hundred percent committed.

I have included, below, a snapshot of my checklist on *How to be the best driver of my passengers*. Some are more serious, while others are light-hearted but most importantly, I grant them all the same importance and attention.

- Be silent when listening and avoid the urge to want to jump in and fix everything. I must admit that as a coach this can be difficult, but I know that my passengers need Clare-Ann the friend and not the therapist!

- View friendship as a gift and never a chore or a duty. When the latter becomes a regular thought pattern, it's a definite sign that it's time to change course or snuff out the tribal flame.

- Every now and again, I will send a quote, a message or write a letter to my passengers, expressing my gratitude of them and the friendship we share.

Almost three years ago, when the idea of writing this book presented itself, I bravely asked my passengers for their support. I designed a two-day workshop, containing similar content to what is presented in this book and invited my passengers over to my home. They were my guinea pigs of sorts, to road test the concept behind this book and provide me with honest feedback.

Their input was invaluable over those two days and provided me with the strength to attach wings to my words and ideas and set them free. I dedicate this book to them, and in turn to all the women who hear its roar and feel its power.

How Do I Find My Tribe?

I often ponder the saying, *I wish I knew then, what I know now*! I guess that's the mixed blessing and frustration of hindsight. I don't believe that I truly understood, nor appreciated the importance of a connected tribe until I hit a wall of realisation in my mid 40s.

Up until then, I had a selection of friends, but I felt restless and longed for a sense of belonging. I enjoyed their company, but there was no deep connection. To be honest I felt like I was deeply drowning instead of blissfully floating.

I used to admire other tribes from afar and sometimes dabbled in their circles, but always knew deep down that I was like a gypsy, just travelling through.

It wasn't until I embarked on a brave and personal expedition to go and find myself, that I gained crystal clear clarity around friendships and, more importantly, about myself. To find your tribe, I encourage you to consider some of the follow suggestions:

1. Martha Beck, author and life coach, cleverly reworks the question *Who am I?* to create a powerful statement worthy of consideration: *What are you?* When you can confidently answer this question, then you are one step closer to projecting your authentic self vibe, which will attract the vibe of potential passengers.

2. Join groups, clubs, communities to find your like-minded people. If you believe that there are others who share your interests, your talents and your gifts, then go out and find them. Chances are, you will have more luck finding them in places which nurture your skills, your talents and your gifts.

3. Be patient and remember that finding your tribe can take time but as English poet Lady Mary Montgomerie Currie said, *good things come to those who wait.*

Average Of The Five People

American author and motivational speaker, Jim Rohn, suggests that we are the average of the five people that we spend the most amount of time with.
His belief is that the people we surround ourselves with are the ones most likely to assist in shaping us; our behaviour, our conversations and often where we choose to focus our energies.
Rohn is suggesting that if you were to choose at random, one of the five 'regulars' in your current life, there is a high chance that you share similar qualities, beliefs, morals and standards, as them.

Dr David McClevand of Harvard supports Jim Rohn's belief that you are the average of the five people you spend the most time with, based on his research in social psychology. He believes that our tribe can determine as much as 95 percent of our success in life.

Unfortunately, this percentage influence can also be applied to the failures in our life, as a result of associating with people who don't share similar ethics, morals and values. One of my favourite quotes illustrates this perfectly. It's one that my father used to persistently remind me of: *"If you lie down with dogs, you get up with fleas."* Whilst I admit that I never truly understood as a child what my father meant by this expression, I gathered that friendship choices were important.

Hitchhikers

While you're travelling along in your Kombi, with or without your passengers, you may feel compelled to stop and pick up a 'hitchhiker', a new acquaintance of sorts. For reasons sometimes beyond your understanding, your hitchhiker crosses your path and decides, maybe by mutual consent, to stay for a while.
The random meeting and inclusion of the hitchhiker may add spice to your trip, fill the silence with pleasant conversation and also provide the sweet treats at each fuel stop.

Even if your meeting was by chance, you may feel an instant connection and secretly hope that they get comfortable in their seat and enjoy the remainder of the ride.

However, for all the benefits that they may bring to your trip, they may be tuned into a different radio frequency and create an uncomfortable, even unbearable, buzz. Similarly, a short or long-term friendship may reach a point in your journey that's stale and a considerable irritation. If this is the case, I hereby grant you permission to lean into the discomfort, to pull over at the next available spot and bid each other a fond farewell.
Like any relationship, a friendship rides a rollercoaster of ups and downs, which is perfectly normal. However, when a member of your tribe contributes very little to the friendship and depletes your energy reserves, it's time.

There will always be people who want to hold you back, just as there are those who wish to propel you forwards. Don't fall into the trap of letting friendships rely solely on convenience and/or obligation.

Be consciously aware of the give and take of friendships. In order to endure any journey, you and your passengers need to be comfortable and thriving in an environment where there is a playful tug of war between give and take.

When I first heard the saying friendships are *there for a reason, a season or a lifetime*, it made it easier for me to understand the role of friendships in my life, as well as helping me come to terms with the ending of mutual friendships.
Be prepared to extinguish the flame of some friendships and send them off with wishes of love and light!

Ignition Exercise
Review Your Tribe of Five

I would like you to now set aside some time to complete a tribe review and write down the names of the five people that you generally spend the most amount of (face to face, phone or online) time with each day, week or month.
Obviously, family will feature predominantly in your top five, but delve further and focus on the people who you hang out with by choice. I encourage you to take a moment to really think through the members of your tribe.

Don't get too bogged down or too despondent if you are unable to fill all five spaces. Remember that we are all unique and have different needs and wants. You may be happy with one loyal passenger in the Kombi, a co navigator to sit by your side.
Or you may seek a Kombi full of activity and energy, finding joy in the knowledge that all available seats are occupied by your tribe.

Under each tribe member's name you can jot down what you love and admire most about them. Perhaps the qualities that you record are at the core of your connection and explain why they have been invited aboard your Kombi and into your tribe.

1. _____

Qualities _____

2. _____

Qualities _____

3. _____

Qualities _____

4. _____

Qualities _____

5. _____

Qualities _____

What did you notice, discover or reaffirm while listing your five people?
_____
_____
_____

Were there any surprises?
_____
_____

To ensure an incredibly memorable journey, you need to make room in your Kombi to accommodate your tribe and be prepared to cater for their individual needs.

What Do I Do With My Tribe?

When you have found your tribe, you will more than likely create pockets or slabs of time to enjoy their company. You will happily prioritise your diary to schedule catch ups. Time will possibly fly when you are together and seem effortless. You will treasure these precious gems of time and hold a permanent yard stick for measuring future experiences with friends and acquaintances outside your tribe.

One of the highlights of spending time with your tribe is that you can simply be together without the need to fill the time with activities and chatter. Being able to sit in comfortable silence or let your hair down and giggle like school kids is also wonderful.

Surround yourself with the people you most admire. In doing so, you can accelerate your personal growth and either establish or consolidate lifelong friendships. Standing back and admiring your tribe should fill you with pride and reassure you that they are an extension of yourself and a perfect reflection of your soul.

Be sure to welcome your tribe with open arms and love them unconditionally, ensuring that they know that they are appreciated.

And lastly, ask yourself the two following questions:
1. Who do I spend the most amount of time with?
2. Who are the people I most admire?

If the answers to both these questions are the same, then you have more than likely found your tribe. Congratulations, you have hit the friendship jackpot!

Trip notes

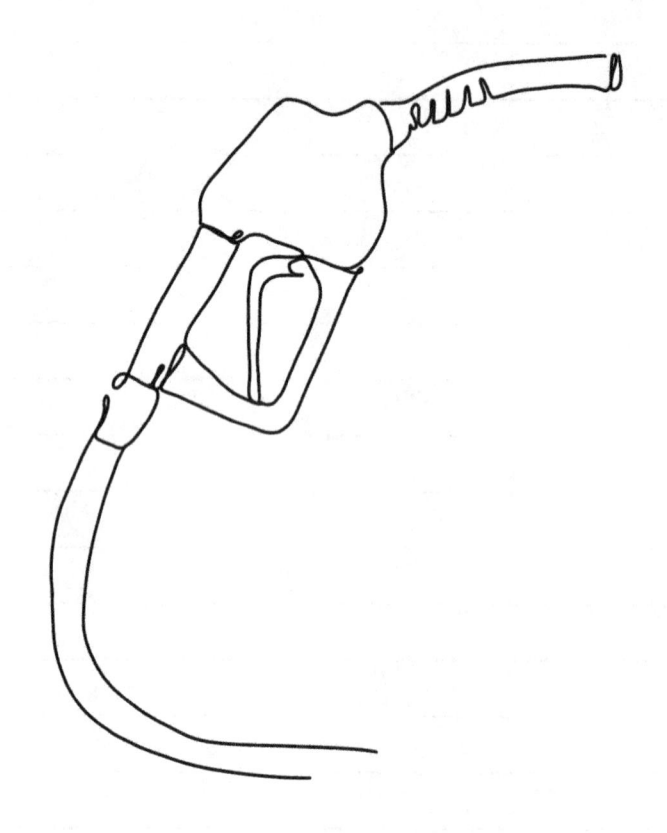

*Create balance, feel your soul,
fuel your body, expand your mind,
strengthen yourself.*

UNKNOWN

The Fuel

The Fuel

I awoke from my light sleep, jumpy at the sound of my newborn son's hunger screams. The cheap baby monitor which had assumed residence on my bedside table 16 days earlier, was quickly becoming my enemy. Isaac's room was next to ours, and while I couldn't justify the need for a monitor, I religiously turned it on nightly.

His restlessness increased, as I willed myself to climb out of my bed and head towards his room for his second feed that night. I was tired, but no more tired than usual, after all, I was a mother of a two-week-old.

Each day had blurred into the next and sleep deprivation was my new form of torture, only eased with caffeine and spasmodic naps while Isaac slept. I made my way down the four wooden steps towards his bedroom. I was grateful for the proximity of his room to ours. I pinched at my left arm, trying to alleviate the pins and needles that had an increasing hold of my upper arm.

I opened the door to the dimly lit nursery. I gathered my son into my arms and cradled him closely to my breast and made my way towards my beloved antique rocking chair. His muslin wrap carried a newborn smell, which I believe should be bottled and distributed, marked as 'captured bliss'.

He fed like the perfect angel that he was, settled and content within his mumma's arms. I shifted uncomfortably throughout the feed, trying to deal with the numb feeling, which was now starting to irritate me, and was slowly making its way up my left leg.

I rewrapped Isaac in his muslin wrap, pressed a warm kiss upon his forehead and placed him into his cradle. I returned to my bed and as I pulled the sheets up over my body, I reached for a sip of water from the glass on my bedside table. I needed to quench my thirst and alleviate the headache that was starting to travel across my forehead.

I drifted into a deep sleep, blissfully unaware of the developing stress that my precious brain was enduring. Isaac was a wonderful sleeper, a welcome change from my firstborn, Isabelle, whose body clock resembled that of a newborn in the Northern Hemisphere.

My husband woke me from my stolen hours of sleep to say that Isaac was stirring for his morning feed. The heaviness in my head felt like I had been hit by a truck. Nausea swirled heavily in my stomach and surged into my throat begging to be released. If I didn't know better, this could have been the taunting reality of a severe hangover from an indulgent night of mixed celebratory drinks. But I hadn't had a drop of alcohol the night before and I now started to listen to the roaring rumbles within my body.

As it was only days before Christmas Day, I spent a lazy morning juggling snuggles with Isaac and wrapping the assorted presents which spread out on our dining table. As I tore off strips of sticky tape and placed them along the edge of the table for ease, my left hand jerked sharply, in a spasm that I had never experienced before. It was enough to freak me out and made me realise that my body was sending me a message and I needed to listen.

The persistent headache, the rolling nausea and now my spasming hand, were indicators that I could no longer ignore. I called my mother, asking her to drive me to our local medical centre. I just knew that my body was under siege, and I needed to rescue her. Two more seizures followed in the waiting room of the surgery; one in my left hand and then the next in my neck.

The last seizure projected me forwards and onto the carpeted area of the waiting room. I eventually came around and found myself on the doctor's examination bed, with no clue of how I ended up there. His words were confusing, but his tone was kind as he reassured me that I was in safe hands.

The details of my transfer from the surgery room to one hospital and then another, are vague recollections. However, while in transit between hospitals, I vividly recall witnessing the third seizure with my husband, as the electric currents traversed my left arm, crossed my chest and disappeared. Our dropped jaws were noticed by the medical staff who were quick to update us that the ambulance was on its way.

I was diagnosed with cerebral venous sinus thrombosis which occurred in my superior sagittal sinus, the main vein running from the front to the back of my brain. It serves many a purpose, but the medical jargon confused me.

Simply stated, it is a rare event, involving the clotting of blood in the cerebral venous sinuses, occurring more often in women and affecting five in one million people. As I was postpartum, (the period beginning immediately after the birth of a baby when the body is returning to its non-pregnant state), I was in one of the highest risk groups. I later learned that the headaches and seizures were two of the most common symptoms.

Two weeks spent in hospital on specific anticoagulant medication, and daily blood tests eased the pressure on my brain, dissolved the clot and I was eventually discharged to return to my busy life. Bearing nothing but insignificant scar tissue damage within my brain; I was one of the lucky ones!

Thankfully, I enjoyed a full recovery and while the events around my medical episode scared the hell out of me, I have learnt many valuable lessons. Life is precious; it literally is an interwoven connection of muscles, bones, blood, air and heat. We are the best listeners of our body. We know her well. We know what fuels her and also what drains her. However, we need to be silent and aware in order to hear her, especially when she is suffering.

Intuition was my saviour that day and continues to be my true GPS; guiding me towards the safety ramp and fueling a more committed approach to conscious living.

Choosing Our Fuel

Choosing the right 'fuel' for our body is just as important as selecting the correct fuel for our Kombi. Just as we are spoilt for choice with petrol, diesel or LPG for the Kombi, we are presented with daily choices to make regarding the best fuel for our bodies, minds and spirits. The choices we make around the *fuel* we consume directly influence our physical, mental and spiritual wellbeing.

We all have basic survival needs to thrive in this life.

Perhaps the table below can be a gentle reminder to ensure that you are at least addressing the basics. Any measures above and beyond this, creates space for possibilities and opportunities to further fuel your overall wellbeing.

BASIC SURVIVAL NEEDS		
BODY	**MIND**	**SPIRIT**
Food	Sleep	Touch
Water	Stimulation	Connection with self
Oxygen	Relaxation	Connection with others
Sleep	Exercise	Connection with nature
Shelter	Socialisation	Connection with the universe
Exercise	Healthy diet	Reflection

One of my treasured passengers, Jodie, shared her thoughts with me on the importance of one of our basic core needs; human touch and its relevance for human survival.

'To observe the relevance of touch one need only
turn to a mother and newborn baby. A baby is
whisked from the womb and nestled straight
onto the new mother's grateful chest. It is here,
during this first touch, the mother and child begin
to bond on a whole new level. This skin to skin touch
begins to regulate the baby's heart rate and it calms
and relaxes both the mother and babe.

When humans touch one another the hormone
oxytocin is released by the brain. This hormone aids
in relaxing the nervous system, creating feelings of
calmness, joy and love.

Adults too, thrive on touch. Healing touch, from
say a massage therapist or the like and is recognised
as the oldest form of medicine. It's universal.

Loving touch releases feel good hormones, it is said
to improve the immune system and assists in general
health and wellbeing.

An extended hug is recognised as relieving
symptoms of depression.

Single adults and the elderly can crave human
touch as they may not come into physical contact
with others on a regular basis. My dear friend's
grandparents had never been separated until her
grandfather, Pete, was dying in hospital. Due to his
wife, Ray, having dementia the doctors thought it best
she didn't see Pete in such a state. It wasn't until the
family convinced the doctors to allow Ray to see her
dying husband, that Pete was able to relax and pass
peacefully holding his wife's hand. It wasn't until
Pete felt the familiar touch of his beloved wife that he
was able to pass peacefully into the next realm.'

Maintenance Of Your Body, Mind and Spirit

Routine maintenance of our Kombi as well as ourselves is crucial for us to stay in great condition and perform at our ultimate best. Like our Kombi, our bodies are machines and require regular check-ups and check-ins. Most of us have our vehicle's service history stowed comfortably in the glove box. It is there as a record of the servicing that has been done.

Strangely, the same is not necessarily so in terms of keeping a record of the servicing of our own bodies. Randomly used journals, diaries and calendars may offer some resemblance, but for me, I rely purely on my mind to keep a record. You may need to schedule regular 'maintenance' appointments in the form of visits to the hairdresser, podiatrist, beautician, masseurs and yoga or meditation practices.
Speaking honestly, I know that I am more inclined to adhere to the mechanical servicing needs of my Kombi than that of me. For me, it's been a work in progress, learning to prioritise my physical, mental and spiritual needs before all else.

I now believe that I'm a far more effective and loving human being when my overall wellbeing is healthy and thriving. I'm ready to receive the day when I'm physically strong, mentally focused and spiritually grounded.

Ignition Exercise

What's Your Regular Maintenance Routine?

Write down any regular 'maintenance' appointments that you prioritise, to nurture your physical, mental and spiritual wellbeing? What is it that you do? How much time do you devote to it? Why is it important to you?

_____

_____

_____

Fuel Light

When you are running low on fuel in your Kombi, the fuel light will illuminate, drawing your attention to the need for action. In addition, there may be a special feature to inform you of how many kilometres you have left before your fuel tank is empty. Intuition is our fuel light, warning us when our energy levels are depleted and when we are dangerously close to mental and physical exhaustion.

Unfortunately, we aren't always privy to the length of time remaining, before we finally burn out. This is even more reason why we need to be in tune with ourselves; being proactive rather than reactive.

> **Intuition is our fuel light, warning us when our energy levels are depleted and when we are dangerously close to mental and physical exhaustion.**

When it comes to our general health, diet and exercise generally come to most of our minds. However, good health involves more than just our physical body, it is about maintaining a healthy balance between our body, mind and spirit. By nurturing our whole self, we are making a conscious effort to attend to our physical, mental and spiritual needs.

If I have learnt anything over the years about my body, mind and spirit, it is the powerful impact that stress can have upon me. Despite the obvious physical signs from stress, it has always weighed me down mentally and effected my spiritual wellbeing.

With many failed attempts at gym memberships, personal training sessions and self-initiated fitness plans, I've often fallen short of ways to refuel my body.
My fitness goals have revolved predominantly on improving my general health and wellbeing, with muscle development and toning an added bonus. Gyms have always been too busy, too cliquey, too expensive, too unhygienic, too something.

I could never pinpoint the problem; I never sustained a routine for longer than six months. That was until I tried one more desperate attempt in July of 2019 to join a fitness centre, 30km from my home. I arranged a tour of the centre, which I basically chose from its outside appearance.

Knowing full well the harsh critic that I was, I tried to keep an open mind as I was shown around the weight and fitness rooms, pool deck, cafe and change rooms. I instantly knew that this was the space for me, for they had me at *welcome*! as I walked past reception.

As the adage goes, it's not what someone says or does, it is how they make you feel, that is what you remember most. I felt comfortable in the space, like I was about to be a part of something wonderful. My surrounds were light and airy and surprisingly, there were no lingering wafts of sweaty bodies and clammy change rooms. The employees looked happy, as did the members, as they quietly worked through their personally designed programs. The branding of my shoes and the labels on my gym clothes meant nothing in this space.

And so, without any hesitation, I signed up!. As members, we were united with a common purpose and that was to improve our overall health, fitness and wellbeing. I can proudly boast I have been an active member of this same centre for three years and attribute it to refueling all aspects of my total wellbeing.

Maintaining Our Bodies

The body of the Kombi is the chassis upon which the parts are assembled. A solid frame becomes the body to house the systems which will drive you towards your destination. So too is your body, a home to house your mind and soul.
Be the architect of your body and shape its structure according to your personality and character. Develop a uniquely strong home, which your mind and soul will seek refuge and comfort within.

Listening To Our Bodies

Listen to your body! We often hear this simple phrase thrown around. But what does it mean? And how do we do it?

I know for me, when I suffered the stroke in 2002, the nausea and headaches that I was experiencing were like nothing I had ever felt before. Being raised by two resilient and healthy parents meant that feeling sick was a mere inconvenience and a nap was the recommended course of treatment. I guess within the 'toughen up' attitude, I was fortunate enough to have avoided hospital visits and I never really had a family doctor until I fell pregnant with my daughter in 1999. For me, it was easy to listen to my body because it rarely cried wolf or entertained hypochondria! I felt that I knew my body well and although it was suffering, I was able to act quickly and potentially prevent any further damage to my brain or self.

There seems to be boundless ways to fuel our physical wellbeing, both indoors or outdoors, free or inexpensive, low or high impact, competitive or not, career or leisure focused, individual or group based. There is no doubt that we are spoilt for choices to fuel up, leaving us with few excuses and reasons to not strengthen our priorities around the regular maintenance of our bodies.

Being mindful of the fuel we choose to use in our bodies will significantly impact today, tomorrow and our future. Feel free to add your own ideas to either column.

FUEL TO ENHANCE THE BODY	
FREE	**INEXPENSIVE**
Bike riding, walking, swimming	Gym membership
Healthy cooking and eating	Dance classes
Dancing	Yoga
Sleeping	Sport
Gardening	
Yoga	
Relaxation	

Your body is your home and because you spend your whole life living in it, you need to ensure that you keep it well maintained. It needs to be physically strong to see you through the tough travels, even when you're oblivious to the strain that's happening under the bonnet.

I remember as a 17-year-old acrobat, being at the absolute peak of my physical health. I was juggling my HSC and three to four hours of intense training a day. I knew that I was burning the candle at both ends, but relaxing my focus and commitment wasn't an option.

The elusive dream to represent Australia in Sports Acrobatics was so close that I could taste it, and it drove me to be stronger, braver and better. My coach, who I despised with every ounce of my being, teasingly dangled the carrot so closely before me, that I became hungry for more.

My body endured physical pain and borderline torture during training sessions, both in the weight room and on the training room floor. The words of my coach still haunt me now as they would drip from her mouth, landing on my exhausted body as it struggled to draw on depleted vessels of energy. "You'll never be as physically fit as you are right now and for that, you will one day thank me!"

Ironically, I did just that! I thanked my coach, who at the time I felt had stolen so much from me physically and mentally. But in essence, she had given me the strength to survive the potentially life-threatening medical episode I experienced in 2002.

The neurologist who diagnosed me with cerebral venous sinus thrombosis suggested that the unusual absence of side effects and my almost certain full recovery was a direct result of my body's physical health and resilient nature.

During the two weeks that I sat in the hospital waiting for my INR levels, (International Normalised Ratio test measures the time for your blood to clot while on blood thinning medicines), to reach a reading of two or higher, I contemplated many things. I had plenty of time to reflect on my life pre stroke and set about making plans for my post stroke life.

Overwhelming gratitude swam through my veins and I had so much to give thanks for, that I would often just get lost in the joy of counting my lucky stars. I don't know about you, but when I'm lost in a moment and digging deeply, I'm blown away with just how amazing the human body is and continues to be.
The physical appearance of our body is one thing - it's like the bodywork of our Kombi - but what it is capable of doing, sometimes defies logic.

Our body forms the physical framework – what's under the bonnet - with which our muscles, nerves and various systems sit within. Similarly, the Kombi is composed of individual parts, which work as systems to ensure the safe and smooth performance of the vehicle and a safe ride on this road called life.

Maintenance Specialists

We have vehicle specialists, otherwise known as mechanics, to take care of the various systems of our Kombi. We trust their knowledge and experience to maintain our vehicle's performance, ensuring its reliability and longevity. Who then do we entrust for the maintenance of our own body, mind and spirit?
We have doctors, specialists and trainers to rely upon to reboot and rebuild our systems when they fail, but predominantly the onus falls upon us. Therefore, we need to develop simple, yet effective daily routines to keep us happy, healthy and productive machines.

Gratitude and Giving Thanks

I am grateful that my body is healthy and strong. There have been a handful of occasions throughout my life when I have experienced the most incredible admiration of my body and its abilities. Two textbook vaginal births were the most profound inner and out-of-body experiences for me. Theoretically, I could comprehend my body's ability to produce such divine human beings, but I was almost dumbfounded by my body's ability to prepare, produce and recover, after such an ordeal.

Ignition Exercise
Reflect on Your Amazing Body

If I can please indulge you in a moment of gratitude, I would like to ask you to reflect for a moment on your own physical health and state of your body.

Write down a few heartfelt words to your body, giving her thanks for the work she does, her courage to show up each day and her relentless conviction.

Dear Body,

_____
_____
_____
_____
_____
_____
_____
_____
_____
_____
_____
_____
_____
_____

Mind Matters

The mind is like the technology which regulates the components to ensure optimal performance of the Kombi. The mind is such a powerful tool and a brilliant source of hope, direction and personal fulfilment.

I believe that the best way to fuel my mind is to approach each day, each experience and each decision with the curiosity of a four-year-old. I honour the phrase *If you don't use it you'll lose it!*, by regarding my mind as a malleable organ, and one in need of regular stimulation.

However, just as the mind seeks challenges to fuel its strength and sharpness, it also requires times of rest to not only recharge but to process the learnings that each day brings. Alongside the need to want to reach out for a Sudoko or crossword puzzle to complete, so too must we also reach out for the light switch or the power button on our devices.

During the recently forced isolation and social distancing regulations that came about from the Covid-19 pandemic, I treasured so many more things in our new way of life and missed very little from pre-pandemic times. I felt that our little family's bond deepened as we spent quality time in our home and on our property; cooking, gardening, talking, doing jigsaw puzzles and playing board games. I know that I will miss those precious family times, but I will endeavour to encourage and nurture these experiences within our home.

Upon returning to the 'norm': and the more relaxed, yet strict rules, the one thing I was happy to go back to was the gym. Besides the obvious reason of shedding the Covid-19 pounds, I needed mental stimulation. Once on that treadmill, I was able to see clearly what I had missed during the gym's absence from my daily routine. I missed the clarity and direction that came with the rhythmic, uninterrupted twenty minutes or so, in my own zone.

A Mind Under Pressure

Warning signs that our minds are struggling may be as obvious as a splitting headache, insomnia, mood swings or memory loss. However, a mind that is suffering may be suppressing a simmering pool of anxiety, depression and poor judgement. It can become a ticking time bomb, that even the lightest of feathers can trigger.

Just as it's important to listen to your body, I believe that the same applies to the mind. We should listen with both ears and act with one intention; that is to identify the trigger or cause of the troubled mind.

I recently listened to a TED talk given by author and psychotherapist, Amy Morin, where she spoke about becoming more mentally strong. There were three main ideas which resonated with me and were so powerful that I would like to share them with you now. To increase your mental strength, you should:

1. Reduce or eliminate the self-pity parties. Whilst they may be easy to attend, they only serve as a distraction and fuel the pain.

2. Stop the blame game. When we blame others for our pain and suffering, we are handing over our power to them and thus disempowering ourselves.

3. Understand that we are swimming in a sea of endless choices and possibilities. The choices we make should reflect our personal values and circumstances and stand alone, with little influence from comparisons with others.

Below I have listed a selection of ways to fuel that brilliant mind of yours. Feel free to add your own ideas to either column.

WAYS TO FUEL THE MIND	
FREE	**INEXPENSIVE**
Sleep	Trivia nights
TED talks and podcasts	Courses
Reading	Meditation
Documentaries	Yoga
Conversations	
Teaching & learning a new skill	
Board games	
Word puzzles	

Lift Your Spirit

The Kombi's spirit is the natural soul of the vehicle, the patina of sorts. A moment of confession here. I had never come across the word patina, but after seeking chapter inspiration from my son, a self-confessed car enthusiast, he referred to the aura or spirit of a car as the patina.

The scuffs, the blemishes, the incidental scratches become the battle scars, which showcase the remarkable history of the Kombi and the driver at its wheel.
A Kombi exudes a certain sense of freedom and adventure through its patina, and that's the reason why this book uses it as a metaphor.

Fueling my spirit is one of my most treasured pastimes, and one that brings me the most joy and fulfillment. The added bonus is that spirit fueling activities can be as inexpensive as you choose them to be.

Below are some of my favourite pursuits, which contribute to the healthy maintenance of my spiritual needs. Feel free to add your personal ideas to either column.

WAYS TO FUEL THE SPIRIT	
FREE	**INEXPENSIVE**
Walking barefoot in my garden	Yoga
Meditation	Farmers' markets
Jigsaw puzzles, Sudoko	Facials & massages
Country drives	Gym workouts
Reading	Lunch catch-ups with friends
Library visits	Camping
Bike riding, hiking, swimming	Vintage store browsing
Writing (letters, journals, poetry)	Upcycling furniture
Beach visits	Cooking, art & photography classes
Photography	Random acts of kindness
Colouring in	Sport
Stargazing	
Random acts of kindness	
Camping	

As I expressed in the early chapters of this book, my life and the choices I make are fueled by several underlying values; kindness being the most revered. To fuel my spirit, I surround myself with kindness and people who stand by it and live by it. Performing and experiencing acts of kindness fuels my spirit and keeps me craving more. The more kindness I spread, the more I seem to experience. Fueling my spirit with acts of kindness and inexpensive opportunities for joy is an addiction that I'm happy to possess, and one that I hope will become more contagious within our society.

The Gift Of Giving Without Expectation

In 2008, I came across a quote by 17th Century English writer, John Bunyan, which contained some of the most powerful words I have ever read. He suggested that you have not lived until you have done something for someone who can never repay you. I sat with this quote for months and pondered how I could experience this pinnacle of kindness. It took me roughly 12 months to figure out how I could fulfil that hope.

As a mother of two young children, I often found myself with limited time to indulge in my true love of reading. However, whenever waiting at the doctor's surgery, or for Community Health nurse, I would steal precious minutes to reach for the latest copy of Sydney Child's Magazine.

I found a couple seeking an egg donor in the classified's section of that magazine. With the blessing from my husband, I made contact with the husband and wife and we arranged to meet each other in their home, about an hour's drive from us. The conversation flowed comfortably, as did their gratitude towards the gift of life that I was prepared to give them.

The months that followed on from our initial meeting saw me attending regular IVF clinic visits, having endless blood and urine tests, enduring internal examinations, harvesting multiple eggs, attending mandatory counselling sessions and injecting anticoagulants into my thighs, so I wouldn't suffer another devastating blood clot!

Finally, retrieval day arrived and the surgeon successfully collected 18 eggs from my swollen uterus! The couple drove me home and saw that I was comfortable upon my lounge. They had prepared a meal for Adam and our children, and quietly headed off to their own home. They were no doubt going to celebrate being one step closer to becoming parents.

This story has a beautiful ending and one that even the most eloquent of words can't express. A precious little boy was born in October 2009, who I was blessed to cradle. I saw him as a gift from me to another woman, so deserving of the deliciousness of a mother's love. Through mutual agreement, our families have remained disconnected. However, I will forever hold dear to my heart the words of Bunyan, as I now feel that I have truly lived!

Ignition Exercise

Explore Your Kindness Story

Do you have a story to share from your own personal experience, or that of someone else, about an act of kindness that could never be repaid?

_____
_____
_____
_____
_____
_____

For me, writing this chapter has been the most beautiful of encounters.
I feel that I have come full circle and have experienced multiple revelations along this short writing journey. We live in a free country, where we are blessed with the freedom of choice and the freedom of action. There is really very little that we *have* to do in our daily lives, for we are spoilt for choices each and every moment that we draw breath.

However, to ensure our basic survival, and in turn create a meaningful life, we need to maintain a healthy body, an active mind and a powerful spirit. I have considered which comes first; the body, the mind or the spirit? Like the chicken and the egg, it's an endless cycle which has no real solution.

Instead, it's the perfect trinity between three powerful forces in our life. To forge ahead on any journey, you need all three forces to be in comfortable alignment.

The body is the HOW of the journey and has to be physically able.

The mind is the WHERE and requires a clear and focused windscreen.

The spirit is the WHY and the positive flow of inspiration and motivation.

Trip notes

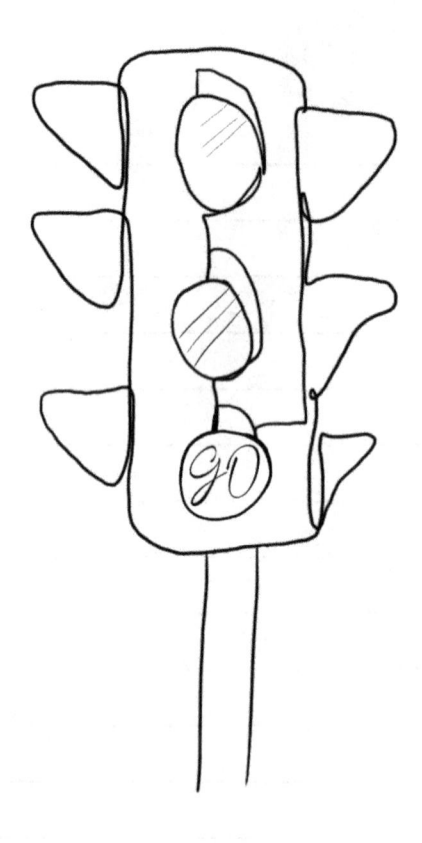

*Give yourself permission to live a big life.
Step into who you are meant to be.
Stop playing small.
You're meant for greater things.*

UNKNOWN

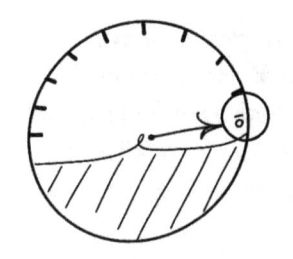

Permission Granted

Permission Granted

It was the morning of my last day of leave when my father gave me a much-deserved kick up the proverbial. He questioned if I had used my leave wisely and whether I had found what I had been looking for? He made it sound so simple, like I had been left with the task of finding a lost sock or the lid to a lonely Tupperware container. I bit down on the annoyance that his words had triggered.

I had sought and was successfully granted two months leave from face-to-face teaching during Term 1 in 2011. The reasons for my leave were numerous, but predominately it was to find my mojo and reignite my passion for teaching.

Two months prior to my leave, my family and I had returned from living in Canada. We had lived in Cochrane, Alberta for twelve months, where I had been involved in a teaching exchange program organised by the NSW Department of Education. The experience had been an incredible adventure for our family, which saw us explore the province of Alberta and pockets of British Columbia during the winter months as well as Italy and the USA in the summertime.

The time we spent away from home provided us with valuable experiences, life long memories, and strengthened our bond as a family. However, when we arrived back in Australia in December of 2010, I was dreading my return to teaching and I knew that I had to better utilise any available leave that I was entitled too.

My enthusiasm for teaching had been diluted by the thoughts of the impending workload in the form of programs, reports, marking, staff meetings and everything *but* what I originally signed up for, face-to-face teaching. I could no longer wear the false mask of pretence, as my students would see straight through its transparent membrane and they deserved so much better.

So, as I stood facing my father, desperately trying to justify my inactions and lack of 'enlightenment' during my leave, I realised that his words were poignant and had pinched a guilty nerve. I potentially had a few hours to figure out my future and make a plan. This was no easy feat, but the road to success never is!

I liked the idea of becoming a life coach but the finer details of how, when and where would overwhelm me and I would retreat back into the comfort of the reliably mundane world of classroom teaching. It was like I was looking at the destination and becoming overwhelmed by the map of confusing trip notes and tangled highways.

Whilst teaching in Canada, I formed a beautiful friendship with a kindred spirit, named Gaynor. She was the yin, to my yang. We spent hours forging a friendship some people spend a lifetime crafting. She was a life coach and was possibly the wisest woman I knew. She walked the walk and talked the talk and I would hang off her every word. She was like my guru and I found the work that she did intriguing.

So, in that moment of *What am I going to do? Who do I want to be?* I found my answer. I wanted to be a life coach, like my best friend, and help people find themselves, just like I needed to. I searched the internet for institutions offering accredited courses in Life Coaching. I found a school in Melbourne, contacted them, felt a positive vibe, and registered there and then to be on a webinar call that evening.

For the first time, in a long time, I was excited and prepared to invest time, energy and money into me. I clearly remember the call. It was a Thursday night and the webinar commenced at 7.00 pm. How do I recall this? I think that when you're desperate and in need of the universe and her guidance, you shift into heightened awareness, and everything seems louder and clearer.

I listened intently to the host of the webinar and scribbled down random points and relevant information as he spoke. The content presented during the first twenty minutes or so was music to my ears. He was speaking my language and if I didn't know better, it may have just been me on the call.

My ears pricked up when he excitedly announced that the next live training intake for their Foundations of Coaching Success, was, in fact, the next day! Of course, there was a catch and an obligatory call to action. I had to register for the three-day training course before 9pm that evening. I stayed on the call to speak with one of the trainers and then we reached the point in the call where I needed to make a commitment.
I froze and balked at the cost of the initial training. It was close to $3 000!
A small deposit had to be secured that evening, with the balance being finalised upon my arrival at the training the next morning.

Respecting my commitment to my husband and the joint decisions we make as a couple, I ran outside to find him. I *was* seeking permission, but I would like to clarify the permission that I sought from him. Adam has always and will always accept that he is married to a free-spirited woman. He has never and will never try to clip my wings or remove them altogether. And for that, I feel blessed.

So, I wasn't seeking his permission to register for the course because random announcements such as that would not surprise him. The permission I sought was in the form of a mutual agreement that the financial investment of our combined money, was warranted. It didn't take much convincing, as Adam could clearly see the glint in my eye, which reflected the spark which had been reignited in my soul. To be honest, he was probably relieved that his wife was back in the game and raring to go. We agreed that I should pay the deposit and finalise the balance the next day at registration. All that remained was for me to thank the universe for showing up at the 11th hour!

The following three days unfolded like a perfectly written script. There were elements of surprise, intrigue, discomfort but most importantly, growth.
That weekend, I mingled amongst people with similar aspirations, all wanting to make a difference in this world. I had a taste of the magical possibilities that coaching presented and I was eager to commence my studies.

It took me twelve months to complete my Certificate IV in Life Coaching, which proved to be a major stepping stone towards where I now find myself. I am the founder of a successful coaching and tuition business which empowers children between the ages of five and seventeen, as well as providing support for their families. As of 2022, Adam and I have been married for twenty four years and one of his most endearing qualities is the belief he has in us. His quiet confidence is threefold; it's in himself, in me and in us. It assures me the freedom that I crave to be myself in a world where I wear many labels and perform many roles. I don't take my responsibilities as a wife, mother, daughter, sister, friend or mentor lightly, but I do deserve the right to also live my life as Clare-Ann, the passionate driver of her own incredible dreams!

As adults, it's estimated that every day we make approximately 100 decisions. The decisions we make may border on the mundane, or venture into the realm of life changing brilliance. Regardless of the intensity of the decisions we make, they should all be seen as opportunities to empower and impact our lives.

The way we choose to act upon these decisions will create lasting memories but on the flip side, inaction may result in unimaginable regrets. When we grant ourselves permission to drive to the rhythm of our own engine, then we are in fact choosing to live a life driven by our core values, vision and purpose.

<u>Personal Definition Of Permission</u>

I would like you to pause for a moment and think about your own definition of the word permission and what it means to you. I would also like you to consider if the word permission has a positive or negative connotation?

Is permission something that you associate with authority, or does it show up in your life attached to mutual respect and mutual agreement?
Encouraging you to think about your own definition may create the unfolding of three scenarios:

1. You may be someone who doesn't require permission from anybody. You may march to the beat of your own drum and that is working well for you, as you journey through this life.

2. You may be someone who relies heavily on the permission from others, including family, partners, friends or society to ensure your personal happiness along your journey. You may choose to play it safe and are the most cautious drivers amongst us.

3. Like myself, you may be green and growing in this department and with the blessing of time and experience, you are learning to sign off on your own permission slips. You happily seek out opportunities and willingly dip your toe into new adventures. However, you sometimes need support from one or more members of your passengers and/or family.

Ignition Exercise

What Does Permission Mean To You?

Wherever you are along the continuum, don't think too much about the words you use for your definition. Just write down the first thoughts which jump into your mind.

Permission, for me, is

_____
_____
_____
_____
_____
_____

Where Independence Shows, Permission Grows

We spend our childhood looking up at the adults who are entrusted to protect us, believing that they know what is best for us. We seek their permission for almost every decision we make, every action we take. Whether it is requesting an extra helping of ice cream, to having a sleepover at a friend's house, to leaving the table.

As teenagers, we begin to test those boundaries and start moving towards making our own decisions, which may or may not prove successful. This period of time, if managed positively by parents or adult role models, becomes a strong foundation for young adults to build their independent permission granting muscles.

I'm thankful that my parents did this well and were able to guide me, from a mutually determined distance. They granted me the space and trust to make my own decisions, without the urge to micro-manage my every move. They granted me permission when I sought it and kept silent when the lessons I needed were more important than the advice they would have given.

Consequences were my biggest lessons and the sjambok, (a heavy leather cattle whip of African origin) which always lay waiting upon the top shelf of our linen cupboard, ensured mistakes were never repeated. Consequences taught me the difference between right and wrong, between pain and pleasure and the inverse shift between cause and effect. Whilst the sjambok was rarely used on me, the silent threat of it was enough to keep me in line and mindful of my potential actions.

As a teenager, I remember slamming bedroom doors, rolling my eyes in frustration and cheekily begging my parents for their permission to breathe! Now, as an adult, all I ever seem to do is grant my permission to my adult children as well as the students I mentor.

Sometimes I joke with my own children and speak with honesty when I say, I have no clue on how to advise them. After all, we have no manual with prescribed rules and regulations. During these moments, I give them the permission to make their own decisions and promise to be there to either celebrate or commiserate on the other side!

Have you ever considered how often we seek permission from those who may also have no idea, no interest and little or no experience?

How strange it is, that we willingly put our potential happiness in the hands of others.

<u>What Are We Waiting For?</u>

Our lives are filled with a multitude of unexpected surprises and challenges around every corner. Just knowing that may be enough to scare us and even prevent us from putting ourselves *out there*. However, as Alice Steinbach author of *Without Reservations: The Travels of An Independent Woman* suggests, by avoiding the corners altogether, we are refusing to live. And if we never turn a corner, we're just driving in a straight line, never making a decision that could ultimately effect or influence the direction of our lives.
I have pondered this question for some time now, and feel that I'm a little closer to answering it. While I can only speak from personal experience and significant soul searching, I feel like I may have stumbled upon some possible reasons behind our inability to grant ourselves the permission we deserve.

We are social beings who cohabit this earth with others, we innately feel a certain sense of responsibility to abide by societal rules and regulations.
But I think it goes even further than social obligations and here are a handful of my beliefs.
As people pleasers, we often seek the approval of others and hence seek external permission to think, decide and act. A number of years ago, I heard the Buddhist belief that you can grow the juiciest peach, but there will always be someone who doesn't like peaches, and this changed my thinking. I now believe that the decisions I make need to be based on my approval foremost, and the approval or disapproval of others is actually none of my business.

The belief of always putting others first is an inbuilt system which some of us need to reboot for our own personal growth. In my early 20s, whenever I thought of myself first and acted upon that, I was always filled with incredible guilt and scolding thoughts of selfishness would ring out in my head. The discomfort that the guilt brought almost always drowned out the slight hint of joy that I had planned on experiencing.

In 1992, I made it through to the finals of an important dance competition - the South Pacific Dance Championships. I was placed against three other dancers and we had performed our solo on the main arena at Homebush Sports Centre. The opportunity had been all I had dreamt about and trained for in the months leading up to the competition.

In addition to the individual competition, I was also competing in the duo section with my best friend of many years. We were the reigning champions from the year before and were hoping to continue our winning streak. Unfortunately, the finals for the duo and solo clashed and were scheduled with only a ten to fifteen minute break between each.

I had to decide, because I knew that the stamina I required for my solo would be depleted if I performed the duo beforehand. I remember sitting in the dressing room alone, trying to make a decision on what to do. I had to weigh up all the possible scenarios, as well as the consequences which would inevitably follow. If I danced both, chances were that I wouldn't take out the prestigious Gold Star award! If I withdrew from the duo, I would selfishly be letting my partner and best friend down.

In that moment, I gave myself permission to withdraw from the duo and focus my efforts and energy on preparing for my solo. I went on to become the Gold Star Solo Champion as well as the Gold Star Champion of Champions. The size of the perpetual trophy I received matched the joy I felt inside. I had made the right decision, I could feel it in my gut and I could see it reflected in my parents' faces.

Sadly, and understandably, my friend was devastated! It was awkward between us for some time afterwards and eventually, we fell away from each other and didn't speak for many years. I finally reached out to her some five years later, and we resolved our differences. Do I regret my decision? No! Would I make the same decision if given the chance again? Yes!

At that moment, where an important decision needed to be made, I trusted my gut and put myself first. No, it didn't please everyone, and some people felt hurt through what they believed was my selfishness. But, at the young age of 21, I learnt about the power of prioritising my happiness before the agendas of others. The win that day was so much more than the two large trophies I received.

Go forth and put yourself first. Your personal growth will thank you and those around you will be inspired by your strength and fearlessness.

Fear Of Failure

I believe that having spent a good part of my childhood and adulthood as a perfectionist, I always hesitated when it came to making decisions, because of an irrational fear of failure.

In my mind, I thought gaining the permission of others regarding the action I was pondering, was a safe option and that I would potentially succeed. What reason would there be for them to deceive me? I also decided that if I failed, I had the safety net of someone else's permission to blame and to catch my fall.
My reliance on blame as a signatory for the permission notes I needed was toxic and misaligned with my values. So, I ditched that strategy and replaced it with independence and responsibility; two mature traits that are crucial features in my permission pack!

What Ifs?

I still surround myself in clouds of what ifs? I pretend that it's my curiosity at play, but truthfully, I know that it is sometimes my self doubt rearing its unwanted head! Now, I simply choose a comeback with its equivalent opposite.

What if I fall? But what if I soar?
What if I fail? But what if I succeed?
What if they don't like me? But what if they love me?
What if I make a mistake? But what about the lesson I will potentially learn?
Now, it's your turn to have some fun and play with the what ifs that dance in your mind!

Ignition Exercise
Explore Your What Ifs

What if I _____? But what if I _____?

What if I _____? But what if I _____?

What if I _____? But what if I _____?

What if I _____? But what if I _____?

What if I _____? But what if I _____?

So, what are you waiting for? If it's the permission to throw a little caution to the wind, then I say permission granted!

Permission To Say No

When you love yourself enough, you will truly appreciate the importance of boundaries and the role that they play in your life. Trust me, I know just how difficult it is to say *No*! My childhood was spent being reminded of how and when to use my manners. I even perfected the obligatory "Yes please", through the falseness of a forced smile. I would always feel the hovering shadow of my parents whenever offered something material or an opportunity.

However, as soon as you start to feel into the comfort of the word *No* and it rolls smoothly off your tongue, you will surely experience change. When we say *No* to the things that we feel won't serve, nurture or challenge us, we are inevitably freeing up the time and space to host the things that will!

A dear friend of mine, who speaks with the honesty of a four-year-old, recently said to me that she now gives herself permission to say no thank you to invitations to spend time with people who are not members of her tribe. She went on to eloquently explain that she believes that 'life is too short to have inbred good manners dictate her movements and time.' I love this!

Permission To Invest In You

I'm curious! How did you come across this book? Was it by chance, by gift or by choice? Regardless of how; we've found each other. Congratulations for the time that you have invested in reading each chapter and hopefully you have completed the Ignition Exercises throughout the book. If so, you have shown that you are committed to you and for that, I raise my glass and cheers you by saying, "Here's to growth, adventure and all that lies between."

Permission To Be Imperfect

Whichever roles or labels we wear throughout our life, we can't help but be a role model for someone. Often, we don't choose to lead by example, but when we are driving to the tune of our own engine, we may unwillingly present ourselves as beacons of hope to those around us.

Because we are human and not mindless robots, it's only natural for us to make mistakes. I feel humbled by those around me who show their human side, warts and all. It makes them more authentic and approachable and for me, more relatable.

As women, most of us need to learn to forgive ourselves for the mistakes we have made and for the opportunities we have missed. Through forgiveness, we learn to feel at peace with our past and embrace all that awaits us. Imagine if you could look into the rear view mirror of your life with a smile of complete acceptance and self love.

I recently enjoyed reading the words of William Arthur Ward, one of the most quoted writers ever in *Quote*, a weekly international publication for public speakers. He denotes that "To make mistakes is human, to stumble is commonplace and to have the ability to laugh at yourself is maturity."
When we finally reach the space in our lives where we are comfortable with our discomfort and perfectly fine with our imperfections, then we happily grant ourselves permission to do whatever the hell we want!

To me, that's liberating and also smells, tastes, feels, sounds, and looks like living. It's like driving down the highway of life with your tribe, your favourite music blasting, and the wind in your hair!

<u>Women Leading By Example</u>

As research for this chapter of my book, I posed an incomplete phrase to a collection of women I knew. Their ages varied as did their careers, lifestyle and family commitments. I asked them to complete the following phrase and I have to admit, their responses didn't surprise me at all.

In fact, as I read through the many responses, I was filled with joy for my sisterhood and the strong-minded women who are driving assertively, in their own lane of life.

I would like to share some of the varied responses I received to the phrase;
I give myself permission to _____.

breathe.	live.	shine.	take myself less seriously.
be me.	be happy.	be curious.	follow my heart.
be thankful.	let go.	say "No!"	trust my gut no matter what!
make time for me without feeling guilt.	not feel the pressure of other's expectations.	do what I can do in whatever time it takes.	make mistakes and move on.
always watch the morning sky open up to a new day.	stop worrying about what others think of me.	rest when needed.	have me time as a mum and not feel guilty about it.
fail spectacularly.	sing.	be who I was born to be.	never apologise for putting my family first.
be satisfied with my successes.	follow my heart.	have the courage to let go of whatever hurts my soul.	be kind to myself.

Ignition Exercise
Write Your Own Permission Slips

Now, it's your turn. I would like you to grant yourself permission to do something; something that you have been wanting to do for a long time (regardless of size, volume, depth). Perhaps, you have been putting off something because the action is dependent on someone's permission.

I grant myself the permission to_____(action) and I acknowledge myself for taking action without the reliance on anyone's permission or approval.

I grant myself the permission to _____(action) and I acknowledge myself for taking action without the reliance on anyone's permission or approval.

I grant myself the permission to _____(action) and I acknowledge myself for taking action without the reliance on anyone's permission or approval.

Permission To Let Go!

Melissa Camara, author of *Permission Granted* encourages us to realise that we are all brave, although scared, we are all messy although real and we are all gloriously imperfect and yet more than enough. I love this!

I believe that once we can learn to speak from the heart and announce to the world, (or even just our reflection) 'Hey! This is me! And watch me go!' then our lives will be filled with purpose and joy, and the ripples we create for others will be empowering.

When we grant ourselves the permission to be who we truly are, our authenticity radar will be powerful enough to attract what we need and with whom we need to share.

So, if you need approval, here it is loud and clear!

LET IT GO!

If it's the approval of others you seek, then stop waiting in line and let it go!

If it's the fear of failure preventing you from setting off on your adventure, then let it go!

If it's the fear of others preventing you from living your life how you choose to live it, then let them go!

If it's the excess baggage that you identified in Chapter 4 that's in your way, then collect it, dump it and leave it behind.

If it's the lack of energy to get you moving, then dig deep and make a plan! Get more sleep, prioritise exercise and nutrition, meditate to keep you focused. Just take one step for yourself!

If it's family, work or life commitments which bring you guilt when you put yourself first, then compromise! Create a balance between work, rest and play, where you benefit.

> **It is time to get out of the breakdown lane. Nothing happens in that space except the looks of pity from passers by.**

Ignition Exercise
Your Final Vehicle Check

It is time to get out of the breakdown lane. Nothing happens in that space except the looks of pity from passers by. Give yourself permission to refocus on the road ahead and the adventures that await. Complete a final vehicle check and answer the following questions.

Who am I?_____
_____(The Driver)

What are my core values? _____
_____(The Driver's Seat)

Where am I heading? _____
_____
_____(The Windscreen)

How will I get there? _____
_____
_____(The Windscreen)

What do I have to let go of? _____
_____
_____(The Baggage)

What are my fears? _____
_____
_____(The Brakes)

How will I overcome those fears? _____
_____
_____(The Brakes)

What sparks joy in my life? _____
_____
_____(The Spark Plugs)

What is my purpose? _____
_____
_____(The Steering Wheel)

Who are my passengers? _____
_____(The Passengers)

How will I nurture my body, mind & spirit? _____
_____(The Fuel)

Letter To Self

So, now there is only one thing left for you to do, and that is to write a letter to yourself.

I want you to approach the letter with all the creative freedom you possess and the courage that I know that you have within. There are no writing scaffolds to follow or content that you must include.

I want you to remember that this is a permission letter, granting yourself permission to be who you want to be, to do what brings you joy and to live a big life. Step into who you are meant to be and remember that you were destined for great things!

When you have finished writing your permission letter, address an envelope and place the letter inside. My suggestion is to pass the envelope on to one of your trusted passengers or a family member for them to keep safe, if and when you shall ever falter and need to bathe in its comfort.
Good luck and enjoy the journey ahead!

Philosopher and writer Ayn Rand once said that if you are seeking the final permission of society before undertaking action, then you are not free, you are more like a slave. Permission from others is not a right they possess, but an act of freedom that you can access.

You may have a tidy collection of permission notes stacked in a very important pile marked *I will get to it one day!* Well, today is the day to drag them all out, brush off the gathered dust and either complete them or cull them.

It truly is that simple!

And as you steer ahead, remember the famous words of Dr Seuss: *Those who matter won't mind and those who mind don't matter!*

Letter to self

From one woman to another ...

Devise, drive and delight in your own brilliance

Permission Granted

xxx

Final thoughts from one Kombi driver to another

Initially, I wrote A Woman's Way for myself; a self prescription of sorts, to help heal my soul and refocus my mind. However, the beauty of this self journey has been, that quite unexpectedly, my musings have blossomed into a manual that I feel will benefit all women, regardless of their circumstances or situations.

As women, I believe that we need to take ourselves a little less seriously and revisit our younger selves and honour the spirit and youthfulness that we once relished. Whilst time has blessed us with storylines upon our faces and syphoned our energy stores, we are blessed with wisdom and intuition.

At the beginning of this writing journey, I set out to answer three simple, yet in depth, questions.

> Who am I?   Why am I here?   Where am I going?

I believe that deep down we know who we are and why we are here but perhaps it's the where am I going that remains somewhat blurry. Through writing A Woman's Way, I feel closer to answering my own three questions. Through the exploration of my childhood and the values instilled in me, I now have a deeper understanding of who I am and what I stand for.

By turning up the volume of my spark dial, I am now more in tune with what brings me joy and keeps me focused. Regardless of the labels I wear, consciously or subconsciously, I feel better equipped now to face my world and contribute in positive and meaningful ways.

My hope for you is simple: that you devise, drive and delight in your own brilliance. We are unique souls; our DNA and fingerprints attest to that.
We were born to stand out, as well as to coexist on this planet. As women, we share the same air and experience the same time. However, the world we share relies on our differences and craves our varying perspectives. This is essential for our survival and for the cycle of evolution to continue.

I'm excited about the journey which lays ahead for you. Whilst mystery may surround the exact route you will follow, the growth you will experience is guaranteed. I applaud your courage, your sense of adventure and most of all your willingness to truly grasp hold of your life and drink in all its magic. If it's permission you have sought well here it is …. I give you permission to be the driver of your own dreams.

This is your journey, driven your way … *A Woman's Way*!

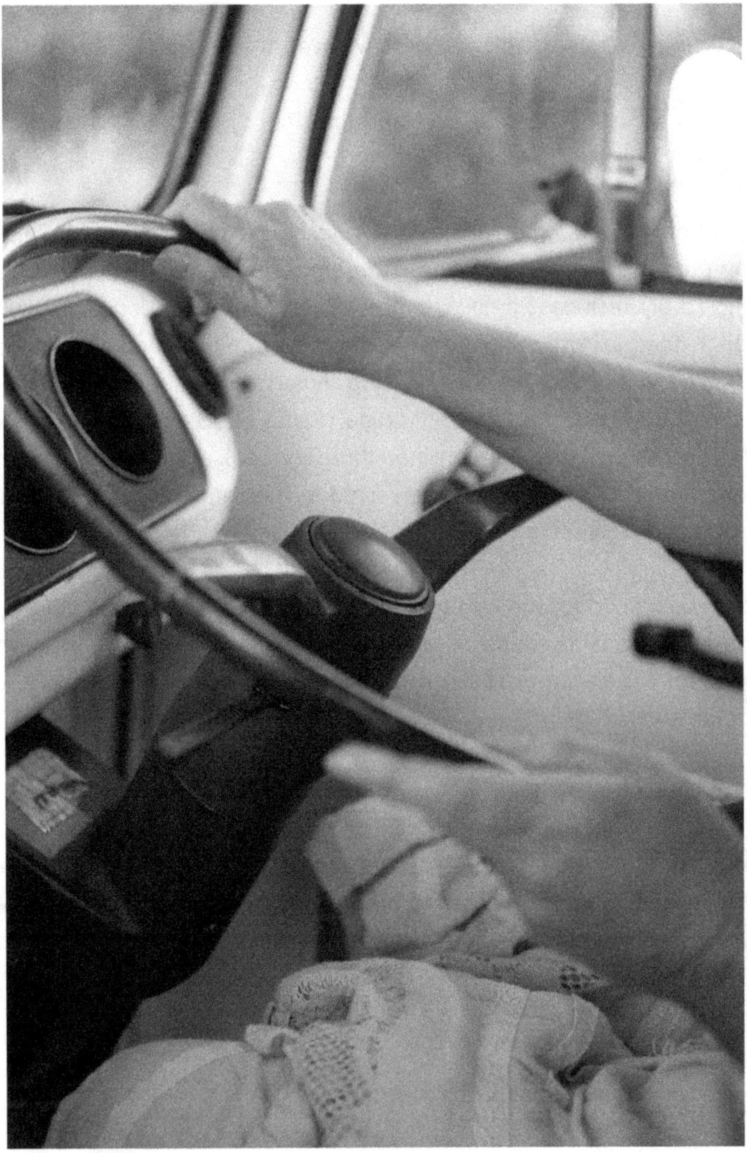

Author Q & A

Why did you write a book about women's self empowerment?

I remember reaching my mid 30s and thinking, "Is this it? Is this my life for the next thirty plus years?"

Don't get me wrong, I had it all! A loving husband, two beautiful children, healthy parents, a secure job and a dream rural property to retreat to. Yet I was incredibly restless. I thought that I wanted more, needed more, when in fact all I needed was silence to gather my thoughts and get out of my complicated way. I searched for reading material, for meditation retreats, for psychologists to heal me, but only came across dead ends and stairs which led me deeper into my head rather than my soul. So, I decided to write, because that has always been my safe house, my antidote to tame my confusion and redirect my focus.

My journal, named Grace allowed me the space to ponder the musings that raced laps around my mind. I give thanks for Grace and the platform she provided for me to compose my thoughts and create the scaffold to structure *A Woman's Way*.

How do you stay motivated and inspired to do the work you do?

Children and the students I mentor provide me with a daily source of inspiration and motivation. They represent the future and provide a perfect blend of curiosity, naivety, hope and possibilities.

What's your wish for people once they've read your book?

My wish for all the women who read A Woman's Way, is threefold. I trust that in reading my book, they will gain clarity in who they are, establish a vision as to where they are going and importantly understand why they are here.

What actions can people take that will help them get started on self empowerment?

Very simple! Just do something! Take a big step, a small step, a sideways step, just take a step that feels like moving forward. Make small things a big priority and celebrate progress, no matter its size or depth.

What is the greatest piece of wisdom you live by day to day?

Leave an imprint of kindness on the people you encounter, so that they too may experience the warmth of human kindness and the feeling of hope it musters.

Acknowledgements

There are many, many people to whom my thanks will never be enough.

To my writing mentor, Emma Franklin Bell, who believed in my vision from the get go and became a loyal travel companion throughout my writing journey. Your guidance and experience gave wings to my words.

Lyndal Edwards, my editor extraordinaire. Thank you for your patience around my punctuation minefield and need for 'perfection'. To hyphenate or not? That will always be the question.

To Hope, you gave my heart's work a title and for that I remain grateful. A Woman's Way you so aptly named, is proof that you have a voice which deserves to be heard!

Thank you Jeff for bringing your incredible gift to me and photographically capturing the pure essence of A Woman's Way.

And then there's the Kombi! My deepest thanks to Matt and Michelle for allowing your orange beast to breathe life into my metaphor for this book.

Jorja, your artwork speaks for itself! Your images are a beautiful accompaniment to my words and their uniquity is preface to your future success as an artist.

My sincere gratitude to to the handful of teachers along the way, who instilled in me a thirst for learning and a yearning for growth. For those who allowed my voice to be heard through written prose and revealed the beauty that words can entomb.

To my tribe who have always been my strongest supporters. As my friends, you are my family and I thank you for seeing me and allowing me to rely on your honesty and loyalty. As passengers alongside me through this journey, I dedicate *A Woman's Way* to you.

To Paul, the greatest friend and human being. We've squeezed a lifetime of incredible friendship into 5 years. You're a blessing to me, our family and this Earth.

Donna, you are one of the strongest women I know! You grace this world with your kindness and generous heart. Of all the labels you wear, I love the ones sister and travel companion the most. You said it best when you said, "I love being a 'Women!'"

Thank you to my Dad for the steady flow of Nancy Drew books, that you knowingly kept track of, ensuring their delivery from your black briefcase was impeccably timed. You introduced me to the world of storytelling and the depths that could be explored. To my Mum, for the selfless sacrifices you have made and the lessons you have taught me, I will forever be in awe and remain indebted.

Isabelle and Isaac; undoubtedly my greatest success! You are the motivation behind what drives me to do what I do, how I do it and why I do it.
My love for you both runs deeper and wider than any other love I know. I love you Belle and Moo to the moon and back and back and back and back ....

Lastly, to my husband Adam; my rock and support. I adore how your unwavering strength continues to chase after my dreams as they dance excitedly through my veins. You enable a life for us; built on love, respect and adventure.
You saw a magic in us from the beginning and poured belief into its reality. Thank you for reminding me to enjoy the view despite the speed bumps, pot holes and detours along our journey. I am forever grateful that you know when to ruffle my feathers and when to preen them so I can soar.

To anyone who has heard me, seen me or ever felt the warmth of my words, this book is a result of how you have made me feel. It is your words of encouragement that have become my inner cheer squad, willing me to keep driving on!

References

Below is a list of the books and websites I have read, visited or referred to in the writing of this book. I trust that you may find them helpful or inspiring in your own personal journey.

Beck, M. (2014). *Finding Your Purpose and Your Power: Rediscovering Your Superhero Self.* [Blog]. Martha's Blog. Available at: https://marthabeck.com/2014/06/find-your-purpose-and-power/ (Accessed 23rd April 2020)

Buechner, F. (1993). *Wishful Thinking: A Theological ABC.* 2nd ed. San Fransisco: Harper One

Bunyan, J. (2008). *Quotes.* [Online]. Good Reads. Available at: https://www.goodreads.com/author/quotes/16244.John_Bunyan (Accessed 9th March 2020)

Camara, M. (2019). *Permission Granted: Be Who You Were Made to be and Let Go of the Rest.* Grand Rapids: Zondervan.

Canfield, J. and Hansen, M. V. (1993). *Chicken Soup for the Soul.* Deerfield Beach: Health Communications, Inc.

Crook, J.A. (2020). *Marcus Aurelius.* [Online]. Encyclopaedia Britannica. Available at: https://www.britannica.com/biography/Marcus-Aurelius-Roman-emperor (Accessed 20th August 2020)

Gilad, Y. (2015). *What Is Patina?* [Online]. Petrolicious. Available at: https://petrolicious.com/articles/what-is-patina. (Accessed 16th July 2020)

Gladwell, M. and Decker, J. (2000). *Tipping Point: How Little Things Can Make a Big Difference.* 2nd ed. Boston: Little, Brown Book Group

Hutton, D. (2013). *Finding your spark.* [Blog]. Balance by Deborah Hutton. Available at: https://balancebydeborahhutton.com.au/finding-your-spark/ (Accessed 17th July 2020)

Lescault, H. (2018). *Focus on Your Circle of Influence.* [Blog]. Franklin Covey. Available at: https://resources.franklincovey.com/blog/focus-on-your-circle-of-influence (Accessed 16th April 2020)

Litchy, J. (no date). *The Power of Giving Yourself Permission.* [Blog]. An Authentic Life. Available at: https://julielichty.com/authentic-life/power-giving-permission/ (Accessed 29th July 2020)

Maraboli, S. (2013). *Unapologetically You: Reflections on Life and the Human Experience.* New York: Better Today Publishing

McFerrin, B. (1988). *Don't Worry Be Happy.* [Online]. Los Angeles: Capital Records - EMI-Manhattan Records. Available at: https://open.spotify.com/album/0L2VM5iuoVRAQXvw2lyRzV?highlight=spotify:track:4v52HuhZqVV0eNpP6vzH5l (Accessed 6th September 2020)

McGraw, P. (2003). *Self Matters: Creating Your Life from the Inside Out.* New York: Simon and Schuster

Morin, A. (2015). *TED Talks: The Secret of Becoming Mentally Strong.* Available at: https://www.youtube.com/watchy=TFbv757kup4&list=PLFZClOS7DCUgBpmxj_kmVjCBaHSCZaMT7&index=7&t=0s

Oyler, L. (2016). *Systems of the Human Body.* [Online]. Body Systems. Available at: https://sites.google.com/site/bodysystemsku/home. (Accessed 13th June 2020)

Reference. (2020). *Who Was William Arthur Ward?* [Online]. Reference. Available at: https://www.reference.com/world-view/william-arthur-ward-c469181241df9d41 (Accessed 29th July 2020)

Science Clarified. (2010). *Automobile.* [Online]. Science Clarified. Available at: http://www.scienceclarified.com/As-Bi/Automobile.html#ixzz6RXwcABSl. (Accessed 13th June 2020)

Steele, J. (2018). *About Us.* [Online]. Available at: https://www.jearlynsteele.com/aboutus. (Accessed 21st July 2020)

Steinbach, A. (2003). *Without Reservations: The Travels of An Independent Woman.* London: Transworld Publishers.

Surfing World. (2019). *The Short History of Kombis.* [Online]. Surfing World Magazine. Available at: https://surfingworld.com.au/the-short-history-of-kombis/ (Accessed 1st March 2020)

The President and Fellows of Harvard College. (2020). *David McClelland.* [Online]. Harvard University: Department of Psychology. Available at: https://psychology.fas.harvard.edu/people/david-mcclelland (Accessed 23rd April 2020)

Tidying Up With Marie Condo. (2018). [Television Series]. Los Gatos: Gail Berman and Joe Earley

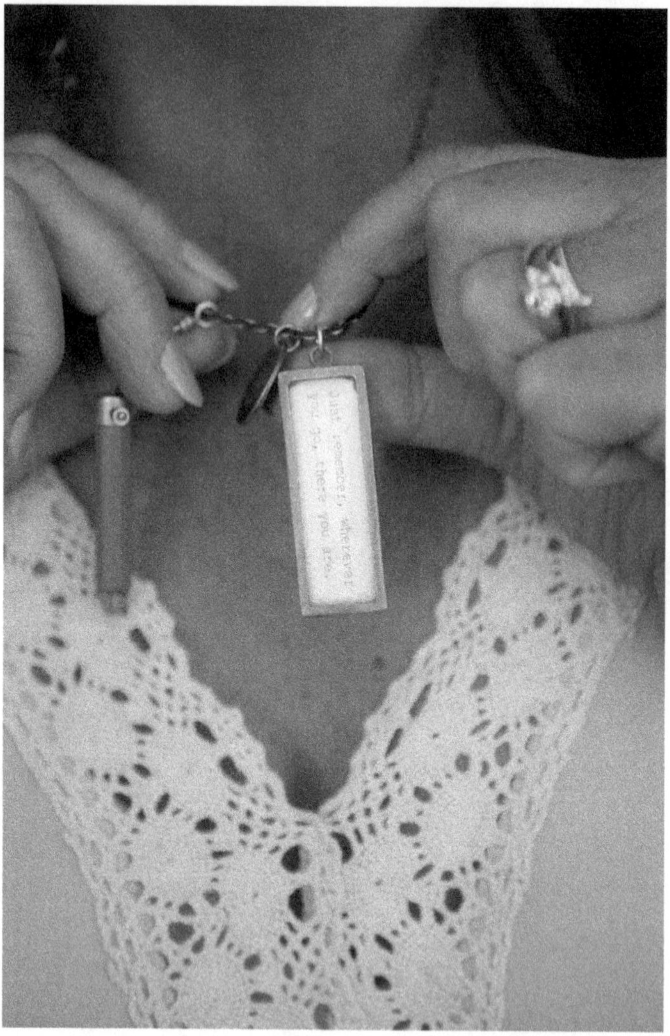
Just remember, wherever
you go, there you are.

About the Author

Clare-Ann Taylor is a teacher, life coach and author of A Woman's Way.
As a professionally trained educator, Clare-Ann has spent the past 28 years empowering children through enhanced learning; and the past decade mentoring women to find their strength in voice and in action, so they may live their purpose.

Clare-Ann has a Bachelor in Education, a Certificate IV in Life Coaching and is an accredited Neuro Linguistic Programming (NLP) Practitioner. She has taught in Australia, Canada and Swaziland, establishing strong cultural connections and mentoring programs.

During her childhood and adolescence, she performed competitively as a dancer and acrobat, appearing on national television and representing Australia in the Sports Acrobatics World Championships in 1989.
Clare-Ann is a lifelong writer who first stepped into the magical world of words in Grade Six.

Clare-Ann lives and works out of her rural property in NSW, Australia.
A country girl at heart, she shares her home with her husband, two adult children, both her parents and all their beloved farm animals.

Born to interracial parents during the apartheid regime in South Africa,
Clare-Ann's family sought a new life in Australia in 1972. Still deeply connected to her roots and heritage, she has returned to her birthplace on many occasions.
In 2017, Clare-Ann visited a rural preschool outside of Manzini, Swaziland. With the generous financial donations made by friends and family, she was able to arrange the installation of a much needed water tank for the children.

Clare-Ann prides herself on her strong work ethic, commitment to personal growth and determination to lead by example. Happiest barefoot in her garden, Clare-Ann has a simple philosophy on life … stamp kindness on those you meet, so its message may be returned to sender!

Connect with the author

🌐 clare-anntaylor.com

📘 facebook.com/clareann.taylor

📷 instagram.com/clareanntaylor

✉ taylor_clareann@yahoo.com.au

About the Illustrator

Jorja Cummings is a full time university student and artist, currently completing her degree in Secondary Education and Visual Arts. Since the age of 15, she has run her own business called Pugs and Pencils; specialising in pet portraits and animal art. Whilst studying over the last few years, she has completed hundreds of coloured pencil portraits for customers all over the world. This is her first job in illustration and she is honoured to be the illustrator in A Woman's Way.

@pugsnpencils

Pugs & Pencils Pet portraits

Be the driver of your own Kombi

Tease your curiosity, deepen your thinking, and empower your life

I've always been captivated by the thought of being a bus driver - more specifically the driver of an iconic Kombi.
There's no deep meaning attached to this desire nor some unfulfilled hippie dreams. I simply just love the idea. Curiosity surrounds the notion of climbing aboard a Kombi, selecting drive and heading off; destination known or unknown.
The sense of freedom excites me; the idea of throwing caution to the wind is often so far out of my view that I need to squint to hold onto its allure.

A Woman's Way is written for women, by a woman who stumbled into her 40's asking "Is this it? Is this as good as it gets?" In an effort to emerge from the tangled mess of intersections, dead ends and detours, A Woman's Way was crafted and now sits in your hands.
All good things take time and this journey that you're about to embark on is no exception. There is no expiry time just an impending departure date.
Buckle in and grip the wheel with both hands. This is quite possibly the most important drive you'll ever take.

This practical and insightful book will show you how to:
- Discover your true self
- Uncover your values
- Prioritise your goals & dreams
- Identify your fears and challenges
- Define your purpose
- Strengthen genuine connections
- Tap into your gifts, skills & talents
- Find what sparks joy within

This book is focused on providing you with a driving manual to guide you towards your happy place. Throughout each chapter there are specific writing exercises designed to help you go deeper into what was covered in that chapter so you unlock more about:

Who am I? Why am I here? Where am I heading?

Clare-Ann Taylor is a writer, teacher and mentor of children and adolescents.
She runs a successful coaching business, empowering children and their parents with the necessary skills and mindset to become life-long learners who create ripples of change on a global scale. As a mother of two, she is passionate about helping women discover their gifts and find their purpose.

Be on your way!

CPSIA information can be obtained
at www.ICGtesting.com
Printed in the USA
BVHW060847140123
656278BV00010B/1261

9 780646 867878